Hot Elements

Hot Elements

GREAT FOOD from The Fire Chef's Kitchen

David Veljacic

DOUGLAS & MCINTYRE

Vancouver/Toronto

Douglas & McIntyre Ltd.
#201-2323 Quebec Street
Vancouver, British Columbia
V5T 4S7

Canadian Cataloguing in Publication Data

Veljacic, David, 1941–
Hot elements
Includes index.

ISBN 1-55054-773-9

1. Cookery. I. Title.
TX714.V44 2000   641.5   C00-910175-6

Editing by Audrey Grescoe
Design by Cardigan Industries
Photography by John Sherlock
Index by Pat Veljacic

Printed and bound in Canada by Friesens
Printed on acid-free paper

The publisher gratefully acknowledges the assistance of the
Canada Council and of the British Columbia Ministry of Tourism,
Small Business and Culture. The publisher also acknowledges
the financial support of the Government of Canada through
the Book Publishing Industry Development Program
(BPIDP) for its publishing activities.

To my mother and father who handed down pieces of heritage to my sister, brother and me.

Writing a book always requires help in one form or another. I had help from many friends and members of my family, and I'm grateful to all of them.

I would like to thank my agent, Carolyn Swayze, who convinced my publisher that I knew how to do more than just barbecue.

Thanks to my mentor, Audrey Grescoe, an editor every writer should have the chance to work with. It seems like we spent hours and hours debating my wording, procedures and techniques.

And to my wife, Pat, who never tired of going in and out of grocery stores shopping for ingredients, and who always managed to make me laugh at failed recipes.

Special thanks to my sister, Sandra Quercetti, for sharing her knowledge of Croatian history and language and for helping prepare some of the dishes for John Sherlock's fabulous photos.

Introduction

Long before I became a competition barbecue chef, I cooked in the kitchens of various firehalls in Vancouver and in the galley of my dad's fishing boat off the coast of British Columbia. Even before that, I had learned to cook as a child at home by watching my mother and my father, both of whom were adept in the kitchen.

My first cookbook – *The Fire Chef* – was a collection of my best recipes for grilling and slow cooking on the barbecue. For this book, I've shut off the burners of my Weber and turned on the elements of my kitchen stove and oven.

You know the old saying about staying out of the kitchen if you can't stand the heat. Well, obviously as a career firefighter I can handle the heat, and so I have no problem about getting into the kitchen and turning it up in a variety of ways. There are several hot elements in this book.

The first is a group of my recipes and two of my wife's that have either won an award or been selected for some other kind of recognition. Blue ribbons are hot in my household.

Another hot element is a sampling of the recipes I learned from my Croatian mother and father. Like yours, my memories of meals at home are heartwarming, but the food we ate was also hot in a peppery, piquant way.

In my other family – the firefighters I work with – I have a reputation as a guy who can cook up meals for special events. I've included my most-requested recipe for firehall celebration dinners – a steamy west coast bouillabaisse – along with some of those fiery curries that firefighters seem to prefer to any other meal.

The hottest of the elements is a chapter with the spiciest recipes in my collection – re-creations of Cajun and Creole dishes I've sampled in my travels. Fire extinguishers are recommended.

Hot has another meaning that has inspired several dishes I've created just for Pat – dishes I like to make when we're spending an evening alone. That's how Pat and I welcomed in 2000 – just the two of us, cooking and eating in a leisurely way over several hours. At 5:30 I opened a bottle of Chardonnay and we had Shrimp with my Seafood Cocktail Sauce (page 157); at 6:30, I served Pat's special

dish, Escargots with Provolone (page 58); at 7:30 I poured
the Merlot to have with Panfried Steak with Glazed Vegetables (page 98) and at 9, it was Vanilla Ice Cream with my
Nectarine Topping (page 144).

I've given you all the hot elements of meals as I make
them – appetizers, soups, entrées and vegetables – as well
as some cooling salads and desserts.

I hope all the elements come together for you so that
you can enjoy a hot time in the kitchen cooking for your
family and friends.

A **CAPTAIN** in the Kitchen

Actually I'm a pretty cool guy in the kitchen. Orderly, prepared, neat – that's my way. Maybe it's the years of job training that have taught me to maintain control under fire.

Keeping your head in the kitchen when others might lose theirs is a matter of preparation and planning. Before I begin to cook, I set the table and get out the serving dishes. I have an array of stainless steel platters that I bought years ago. I like to serve on them because they are easy to clean, they look shiny and people are less likely to try to touch them and so won't get burned if they are hot. I can put a roast on one of those platters, carve it and not lose any of the juices.

I've figured out beforehand how I'm going to arrange the food on serving platters or plates. Restaurants do this kind of plate design all the time; it's not something most people at home handle well in the last-minute flurry of trying to get food to the table while it's still hot.

I've written my recipes just as I would work: all the vegetables are washed, cleaned and chopped, the chicken pieces are skinned and split and the herbs measured and blended before I begin to cook.

Another thing I do before cooking is to get out *all* the pans, utensils and serving dishes I'm going to need. I don't like to be searching through a drawer for a slotted spoon when the fritters need to come out of the oil immediately. Also when my guests are sitting in the dining room, I don't want them to hear me banging drawers and clashing cutlery.

As much as possible, I wash up as I go along. Another firehall habit: because we had only an hour for lunch, we wanted to be able to sit and talk after we'd eaten, so we cleaned up as we cooked. Also, I hate coming into a messy kitchen after the guests have left.

As an example of my style in the kitchen, one of my favourite entries in this book is more a battleplan than a recipe. It's a step-by-step guide to producing a hassle-free turkey dinner. Everyone knows that the last hour of cooking a holiday meal is usually the worst. What with mashing potatoes, making gravy, cooking vegetables and carving the turkey, the cook is usually a wreck and so is the kitchen. My plan gets most of that work done earlier in the day, allowing the cook to join the guests for a relaxed time before dishing up the feast. And believe it or not, if you follow my instructions, you'll have only one dirty saucepan sitting on the stove when you return to the kitchen to clean up.

As for grocery shopping, I do it every day. I always have a shopping list because I always follow a recipe. If I try to find inspiration in what's available at the supermarket, I fail and we wind up going out for dinner.

You won't find me opening the refrigerator door at 6 o'clock, poking among leftover bits of this and that and trying to figure out what I can make for dinner. My mother used to be able to do that; she often made what we called Clean-the-Fridge Soup. But I don't keep leftovers and I believe in cooking with fresh seafood, meat and produce.

While I often can't make a sandwich with what's in my refrigerator, I can always cook up a meal with the staples I have on hand. Some of those are my own preserves, sauces, salsas and other useful components of my cooking. You'll find recipes for many of these standbys in this book.

My Pots and Pans

I don't have many nifty kitchen gadgets. I have a food processor, but it's on an upper shelf and so I only take it down when I really need it. I prefer to chop or mince by hand. It's easier to wash a knife than the blade and container of a processor.

My saucepans, pots and frying pans are stainless steel with heavy bottoms, which I find aid in browning foods and making roux. In my recipes I call for small, medium and large sizes. These are the more precise measurements:

· Saucepans: small (1.5 quarts); medium (2 quarts); large (2.5 quarts).

· Pots: medium (6 quarts); large (8 quarts).

· Frying pans: medium (8 and 10 inches); large (12 and 14 inches). When I call for a deep frying pan, I mean one with straight sides about three inches in depth.

· For deep-frying, I have a pot that is eight inches in height and diameter. About nine cups of oil gives a sufficient depth for most deep-frying.

· I also call for nonstick frying pans for certain techniques. They are good for making omelettes and for cooking things you don't want to brown. In fact, it's hard to brown something on a nonstick surface.

AWARD WINNERS

I've been competing in barbecue and grilling competitions for years, and I've collected my share of trophies. I was among the twenty-four regional winners invited to cook in the Jack Daniel's Invitational BBQ Cookoff in Tennessee, and my wife and I took a first at another contest – Memphis in May – which is the opening event of each season.

I also compete in chili cookoffs. My first was in 1985. After that, I qualified several times for the World Chili Championship in Terlingua, Texas. Among 400 competitors, I've placed in the top fifteen. Chili competitions have two categories: one is for championship chili, which has no meat and no vegetables; the other is homestyle chili. Because most people prefer chili with meat, I've included my winning homestyle chili recipe but omitted my championship chili, which is harder for people to appreciate. I've also given you my wife's winning homestyle vegetarian chili, which fools even determined carnivores.

Most barbecue competitions have side-dish categories. One win that surprised me was at Taylor, Texas. This is a friendly event, probably because no prize money is involved. I entered a pasta side dish that had a white sauce with garlic in it. I was taking a chance because Texans, who were the judges, don't seem to like garlic. But I won the blue ribbon.

CRAB
cakes with red bell pepper sauce

1 lb	crab meat
¾ lb	hand-peeled shrimp meat, minced
1½ cups	fine dry bread crumbs, divided
¼ cup	minced fresh parsley
2 tbsp	minced fresh chives
1	garlic clove, minced
1 tbsp	black pepper
1½ tbsp	seafood seasoning (e.g., Old Bay Seasoning)
1 tbsp	fresh lime juice
2	large eggs, well beaten
4 tbsp	olive oil
3	large limes, each cut into 8 wedges
1 cup	Red Bell Pepper Sauce (see p 153)

I like cooking crab cakes and eating them, particularly for lunch. The sweetness of the shrimp and the tang of the lime juice set my recipe apart and earned it a blue ribbon in a contest in Lincoln City on the Oregon coast.

The Red Bell Pepper Sauce should be at room temperature when you serve it with the cakes.

Pick through the crab meat to remove pieces of shell. Combine the crab and shrimp and gently mix in ½ cup of the bread crumbs. Stir in the parsley, chives, garlic, pepper, seafood seasoning and lime juice. Be careful not to crush the crab meat. Add the beaten eggs to the mixture, mixing well but gently.

Form the crab mixture into 12 patties approximately 4 inches in diameter and 1 inch thick. Gently press each crab cake into the remaining bread crumbs. Place the cakes on a baking sheet lined with wax paper. Cover with wax paper and refrigerate for 1 to 2 hours to give them time to set.

Heat 2 tablespoons of olive oil in a large frying pan. Sauté half the cakes until golden brown on both sides, about 3 minutes a side. Use the remaining 2 tablespoons of oil to sauté the other cakes.

Drizzle equal amounts of room-temperature Red Bell Pepper Sauce on each of 4 plates. Arrange 3 crab cakes on top and circle with lime wedges.

Serves 4

SMOKED SALMON marinated in balsamic vinegar

First published in 1994 in British Columbia Salmon: A Celebration of Paintings and Cookery, *this recipe was later printed in* Woman's Day Magazine, *the* Seattle Times *and* The Vancouver Sun, *which declared it one of their summer favourites.*

Under refrigeration it will keep for up to two weeks.

2 lbs   smoked salmon, sliced ⅛-inch (or less) thick
2   large white onions, sliced very thin
1 cup   olive oil
¼ cup   white vinegar
⅛ cup   balsamic vinegar
1 tbsp   ground black pepper
iceburg lettuce, shredded by hand
ground black pepper
baguette bread

In a one-quart glass or plastic container with a sealable lid, arrange a layer of salmon followed by a thin layer of onion and a sprinkle of pepper. Continue these layers until you have used all the salmon. Finish with a layer of onion.

Blend the olive oil, white vinegar and balsamic vinegar. Pour this mixture over the salmon, making sure it is covered. Seal the container and refrigerate for at least 24 hours. Several times during the marinating period turn the container upside down and leave it inverted.

To serve, place a ½-inch layer of shredded lettuce on a platter or on individual side plates. Remove the salmon slices and onion rings from the marinade using tongs so that some of the marinade remains on them. Arrange the salmon and onion on top of the lettuce and sprinkle with pepper before serving with baguette bread.

Serves 8 to 10

Penne Salad
with PEPPERS, OLIVES and DRIED TOMATOES

2	large red bell peppers
2 tbsp	and ½ cup olive oil
1 tbsp	balsamic vinegar
1 cup	pitted black olives, coarsely chopped
½ cup	minced fresh parsley
¼ cup	oil-packed dried tomatoes, cut into slivers
3 tbsp	dried and crushed red chilies
4	large garlic cloves, minced
2 sprigs	cilantro, minced
2 tsp	ground black pepper (or to taste)
1 tsp	grated lemon peel
½ cup	freshly grated Parmesan
¼ cup	salted pine nuts
¾ lb	penne

Several years ago, my wife and I created this salad for a cruise ship luncheon served to Canadian firefighters who were testing their professional skills at a competition in Vancouver. A few weeks later, we entered the salad as a side dish in a barbecue cookoff in Washington State. It won a blue ribbon.

Lightly toast the pine nuts in a heavy frying pan without oil.

Seed, remove the white membranes and thinly slice the red peppers parallel to the ribs.

Heat the 2 tablespoons of olive oil in a frying pan and sauté the bell peppers until very limp. Remove from the heat, stir in the vinegar and set aside.

Make a sauce by combining the olives, parsley, ½ cup olive oil, dried tomatoes, red chilies, garlic, cilantro, pepper and lemon peel. Toss well and allow to sit at room temperature.

Cook the pasta, drain and place in a serving bowl. Sprinkle with the cheese, add the sauce and toss gently. Distribute the bell peppers and the oil sauce over top and sprinkle with pine nuts before serving.

Serves 6 to 8

Shrimp PERLU with basmati rice

Perlu is a Louisiana style of jambalaya. My version, which contains Italian sausage and more garlic than usual, was chosen for the Gilroy Garlic Festival Cookbook and is one of several of my recipes in that book.

2 lbs	large hand-peeled shrimp meat
2	mild Italian sausages
1⅓ cups	basmati rice
4 tbsp	olive oil
8	large garlic cloves, minced
1 cup	chopped celery heart (the tender, inner ribs)
½ cup	minced red bell pepper
3 tbsp	sweet hot sauce (e.g., Tiger Sauce)
1 tbsp	ground black pepper
¼ tsp	salt

Cook the rice. To keep it warm, place it in a colander over simmering water and cover with foil or a lid.

Prick the sausages and fry them until well browned. Drain off the fat and chop them into ¼-inch pieces.

Heat the oil in a deep, large frying pan and sauté the garlic over low to medium heat for 5 minutes. Add the celery and bell pepper and sauté until the vegetables become limp. Stir in the shrimp, sausage pieces, pepper, salt and hot sauce. Sauté for 5 minutes more. Blend in the cooked rice a little at a time and cook and stir only until the entire dish is heated.

Serves 4

homestyle
chili with ITALIAN SAUSAGE

2	mild Italian sausages
3 lbs	coarsely ground lean beef
2 tbsp	olive oil
3	large leeks, minced
1	celery heart (the tender, inner ribs), minced
6	large garlic cloves, minced
6 oz	chili powder
2 tbsp	cumin powder
2 tbsp	Mexican paprika
½ tbsp	dried whole Mexican oregano
1 tsp	salt
1 can	(28 oz) plum tomatoes, drained and chopped
1 tbsp	beef bouillon granules
1 tbsp	chicken bouillon granules
4–6 cups	V8 Vegetable Cocktail
2 cans	(14 oz each) pinto beans, drained
1	large white onion, minced
1	large green bell pepper, minced
	white pepper

My homestyle chili recipe has won many events in Canada and the United States.

Ask your butcher to grind the beef coarsely so that you will be aware of the small pieces of meat when you are eating the chili. Use white pepper to bring up the heat without changing the flavour. And yes, I use six ounces of chili powder by weight, but see my comments on chili powder on page 159.

Fry the sausages well in a large pot. Remove with a slotted spoon and set aside. Remove all the fat from the pot.

Heat the olive oil in the pot and sauté the leeks and celery until very limp. Add the garlic and sauté for 5 minutes. Add the beef and cook until well browned. Stir in half of the chili powder, cumin, oregano, paprika and salt. Add the tomatoes, beef and chicken bouillon granules and enough V8 juice to create a sauce with a nice consistency. Cover and simmer for 20 minutes.

Cut the sausages in half lengthwise and then into ⅛-inch slices. Add them to the pot with the remainder of the spices. Simmer for 10 minutes. Stir in the beans, minced onion and bell pepper. Add white pepper. Simmer covered for 5 minutes. Allow to stand off heat for 10 minutes.

Serves 4 to 6

PRAWNS & PENNE

HOT ELEMENTS · 8

At a large competition near Austin, Texas, I submitted this white-sauced prawn-and-penne combination in a pasta side-dish contest. Most of the other contestants prepared a red sauce without garlic, because garlic is not a common ingredient in Texas. Nevertheless, much to my surprise, this garlicky white sauce won the blue ribbon.

1 lb	fresh prawns
3	large plum tomatoes
4 slices	bacon, chopped
2 tbsp	butter
2 tbsp	olive oil
2 tbsp	flour
1/2 cup	finely minced leeks, white ends only
3	large garlic cloves, minced
1–2 cups	clam nectar or juice
1 tsp	ground black pepper
1/4 tsp	dried and crushed red chilies
5 tbsp	minced fresh parsley
1 cup	whipping cream
1/2 cup	freshly grated Parmesan
3/4 lb	penne

Peel the prawns but leave the tails on.

Fry the chopped bacon until crisp. Remove from the pan with a slotted spoon and drain on paper towels. Discard the fat

Peel, seed and finely chop the tomatoes. (Large, ripe plum tomatoes can be peeled with a paring knife.) Cook them in a small saucepan for 10 to 15 minutes, stirring often. Cover and set aside.

To prepare the sauce, heat the butter and oil in a large frying pan. Sauté the prawns for 3 to 4 minutes. Transfer to a bowl, cover with plastic food wrap and set aside.

Sauté the leeks and garlic in the frying pan until the leeks are limp. Stir in the flour and cook over medium heat for two minutes, creating a light blond roux. Stir in the cooked tomatoes and bacon and slowly add the clam nectar or juice, stirring constantly. As the sauce heats, it will thicken. Add as much clam nectar or juice as necessary to achieve the consistency you prefer.

Stir in the pepper and red chilies. Simmer lightly for 5 minutes. Stir in the cream and cheese and simmer until the

(in a white sauce)

sauce is smooth. You may have to add a little more clam
nectar or juice. Gently add the prawns and 3 tablespoons of
the parsley, simmering for about 2 minutes.

Cook the pasta, drain well and return to the pot. Add
half of the sauce and toss gently. Ladle the pasta into the
centre of a shallow serving bowl. Encircle the pasta with
the prawns and sprinkle it with the remaining parsley. Put
the remaining sauce into a gravy boat and pass it with the
pasta.

Serves 4

Ćuspaj

While I was on holiday in Louisiana, I met a chef at a small café. I told him about a vegetable dish my father used to make, and he suggested I enter it in a local competition. He obtained an entry form and, just as he predicted, the organizers were pleased to have a contestant from faraway British Columbia, and they awarded my entry first place.

I really do mean a tablespoon of black pepper; you may want to experiment with less at first.

¼ cup	olive oil
3 tbsp	flour
1	medium onion, minced
8	large garlic cloves, minced
1 bunch	fresh parsley, minced
2 tbsp	tomato paste
1 lb	frozen small peas
1 tbsp	ground black pepper (or to taste)
	hot water

Heat the olive oil in a heavy medium pot. Stir in the flour and sauté over medium heat for about 12 minutes until you have a mahogany roux. Lower the heat, add the onions and sauté until limp. Add the garlic and parsley, sauté for 8 minutes and remove from the heat. Blend in the tomato paste, return to the heat and gently stir in the frozen peas.

Add ¼ cup of hot water at a time until the sauce is thick enough to coat the peas, but not soupy. Stir in the pepper and simmer for 10 minutes, stirring often.

Serves 4

(Peas in a tomato garlic sauce)

3-blue-ribbon
clam chowder

5 lbs	unpeeled Yukon gold potatoes
1 lb	bacon slices, finely chopped
3	large leeks, minced
2 cups	celery root, grated
10	large fresh okra pods, diced
2 ½ lbs	fresh clam meat
2 cups	clam nectar or juice
1 tbsp	ground black pepper
1 tbsp	seafood seasoning (e.g., Old Bay Seasoning)
½ tsp	salt
¼ tsp	hot sauce (e.g., Melinda's XXXtra Hot Sauce)
1 cup	whipping cream, plus some extra
1	large carrot, grated and chopped
2 stalks	celery, chopped

Chop half the clam meat and mince (very finely chop) the other half. Put all the clam meat into a small saucepan, cover with water and simmer for half an hour. Drain and hold the clam meat, reserving the liquid.

In a large pot cover the potatoes with water and bring to a boil. Lower the heat and cook until they are fork-tender. Drain, reserving some of the cooking water, and allow them to cool. Remove the skins. Cut half the potatoes into 1-inch cubes. Mash the remaining half, using enough of the cooking water to make them creamy smooth.

Boil the carrots and celery in a small saucepan until tender. Drain and set aside.

Sauté the chopped bacon in a heavy-bottomed pot until crisp. Remove to a bowl with a slotted spoon. Sauté the leeks, celery root and okra in the bacon fat for 10 minutes. Add just enough reserved clam liquid to cover the vegetables and simmer for 15 minutes.

Transfer this vegetable mixture to a food processor and purée. You may have to add more of the reserved clam juice to blend it well. Return the vegetable purée to the pot, stir in the bacon, clams, clam nectar or juice and 1 cup whipping

This recipe placed first several years in a row at a clam chowder competition in the municipality of North Vancouver.

Although the recipe seems long, Pat and I have prepared it during a competition in less than an hour.

Instead of cornstarch, I use mashed potatoes to thicken my chowder. That avoids the tendency of chowder to get thicker the longer it stands.

THERE'S MORE · · · >

cream and bring to a low simmer. Stir in the pepper, seafood seasoning, salt, hot sauce and the cubed potatoes.

Gently stir in the mashed potatoes a little at a time. Use just enough mashed potatoes to thicken the chowder. If it is too thick, add more whipping cream.

Stir the cooked carrots and celery into the chowder. Simmer for 5 minutes to heat before serving.

Serves 6 to 8

24-hour cucumber
pickles with chili peppers

5	medium English cucumbers
1	medium red onion, thinly sliced
1 tbsp	celery seed
1 tbsp	salt
1 cup	white vinegar
½ cup	fresh lime juice
¼ cup	raspberry vinegar
2 cups	white sugar
1 tsp	dried and crushed red chilies
2	medium fresh red hot chili peppers, halved lengthwise

Do not peel the cucumbers. Wash them well and cut into ¼-inch slices.

Place the cucumber, onion, celery seed and salt in a bowl and refrigerate for half an hour. Toss several times.

Simmer the white vinegar, lime juice, raspberry vinegar and sugar in a saucepan, heating just long enough to dissolve the sugar. Stir in the dried red chilies, remove from the heat and allow to cool.

Pack the cucumber and onion slices into sterile jars. Slip half a red hot pepper, facing outwards, down the side of each jar. Ladle the vinegar brine over, making sure the contents are entirely covered in liquid. Seal the jars with sterilized lids.

Yields 3 to 4 quarts

One summer, Pat entered these pickles in the preserve category at the Granville Island Fall Fair in Vancouver, adding another blue ribbon to our collection.

Because you don't process these pickles in a boiling-water bath, they are easy to prepare but they must be stored in the refrigerator. They will be ready to eat in 24 hours but do get more flavourful if allowed to sit longer. They can be kept, refrigerated, for up to a month.

Vegetarian CHILI by Patricia

Meat-eaters are often fooled by this vegetarian dish. A homestyle chili, it has won competitions in British Columbia and Alberta. Six ounces of chili powder by weight is correct, but do read about chili powder (page 44).

⅓ cup	olive oil
4	large leeks, white ends only, finely chopped
1	large white onion, chopped
5	large carrots, grated
2	celery hearts (the tender, inner ribs), chopped
8	large garlic cloves, minced
6 oz	chili powder
1 tbsp	minced oil-packed, dried tomatoes
1½ tbsp	cumin powder
1 tsp	salt
¼ tsp	dried and crushed red chilies
2 cans	(28 oz each) plum tomatoes, drained and chopped
4–6 cups	V8 Vegetable Cocktail
1	green bell pepper, finely chopped
1	red bell pepper, finely chopped
1	yellow bell pepper, finely chopped
3 cans	(14 oz each) pinto beans, drained

Heat the olive oil in a heavy pot. Sauté the leeks, onion, carrots, celery hearts and garlic until they are very limp.

Stir in the chili powder, dried tomatoes, cumin, salt, red chilies and plum tomatoes. If the chili is too thick, add enough V8 juice to make an appropriate consistency. Cover and simmer for 20 minutes.

Gently stir in the bell peppers and the pinto beans and simmer only long enough to heat the beans.

Serves 6

FROM MY FAMILY

It's not surprising that the first Croatian communities in Canada, established in the 19th century, were on the Pacific coast. Many Croatians were fishermen and others were miners. British Columbia offered opportunity and employment for both.

My dad's family came from Crkvenica, which had long been a fishing port on the Adriatic. When he arrived in British Columbia in his early 20s, Dad found work fishing salmon and pilchards. It didn't take him long to acquire his own boat. When I was 18, I spent the first of nine years fishing salmon and herring with my dad and six other crew members.

My mother, who was perhaps the more staunchly Croatian, was born in Canada. Her parents had emigrated from Dalmatia, which was once a kingdom and is now a region of Croatia.

My parents met and married in Vancouver in 1937. Like so many emigrant families, mine adapted themselves to Canada but continued to cook the familiar food of home. Eating these meals, I learned Kitchen Croatian – words such as *lonac, rižot* and *lešćo,* and I developed a taste for this hearty and fairly spicy cuisine, with its accent on pepper and vinegar and chilies.

For this chapter, I re-created the dishes I remember best from Dalmatia, Croatia and neighbouring Montenegro. I included one new-world recipe that made memories for my own children.

Batuda

2	meaty smoked ham hocks
¼ cup	olive oil
2½ tbsp	flour
2	large onions, diced
1 cup	diced celery
5	large garlic cloves, minced
1 bunch	fresh parsley, minced
2 tbsp	ground black pepper (or to taste)
3 tbsp	tomato paste
2 cans	(19 oz each) romano beans
3 cans	(12 oz each) corn niblets

Place the ham hocks in a stock pot, cover with water and bring to a boil. Cover and simmer for 2 to 3 hours. Remove the ham hocks and set aside. Strain the stock and place in the refrigerator overnight. Strip any meat off the bones and serve with sourdough bread and a green salad for a great lunch.

The next day, discard the fat and bring the stock to room temperature. Heat the olive oil in a large pot. Stir in the flour and sauté over medium heat for 12 minutes, until you have a dark mahogany roux. Add the onions, celery, garlic, parsley and pepper. Cook for 8 minutes. Add the tomato paste, blending it in well. If the mixture is too thick and will not blend easily, add a little stock. Bring this to a low simmer.

Drain the beans and corn and gently stir them in. Add the ham stock to the pot, covering the ingredients by 1½ inches. Bring to a boil, lower the heat and simmer for 10 minutes. Stir often but gently. Add salt to taste and more stock if it is necessary. Cover and simmer over low heat for 20 minutes.

Serves 8

In the Dalmatian region of Croatia, the preparation of this chowder begins with soaking dried beans and stripping kernels off cobs of corn. I find that canned beans and corn produce a good result.

To transform batuda into a vegetarian dish, replace the ham stock with six to eight cups of vegetable broth. If you are going to use ham stock, prepare it the day before so you can cool it and remove the fat.

I usually make batuda in large quantities and give it to friends and relatives. It freezes well.

(bean and corn chowder)

LONAC

This recipe may remind you of dishes from the American south but its origins are eastern European. In the late 1800s a large group of Croatians settled in Biloxi, Mississippi. Much of their home cooking blended well with the local cuisine and had an influence on it.

Dalmatians usually prepare this dish the day before, allowing the flavours to meld. Serve with cooked cornmeal (see page 130) or rice, and some fresh bread.

2 lbs	whole hand-peeled shrimp
½ lb	lean ham, cut into julienne strips
¼ cup	olive oil
2	large leeks, white ends only, minced
1	white onion, minced
1 lb	fresh okra, cut into ⅛-inch rings
9	large garlic cloves, coarsely chopped
1 tbsp	dried and crushed red chilies
½ tbsp	ground black pepper
½ cup	minced fresh parsley
1 can	(28 oz) plum tomatoes, drained and chopped
4–6 cups	V8 Vegetable Cocktail
	salt

Heat the olive oil in a heavy frying pan. Sauté the leeks and onion until limp. Stir in the okra, garlic, red chilies and pepper and sauté for 5 minutes. Add the ham, parsley and tomatoes, sautéing for 5 minutes more.

Okra will naturally thicken the sauce. Add enough V8 juice to make and keep it smooth. Simmer on a low heat for half an hour, stirring several times. Fold the shrimp into the sauce, cover and simmer for about 8 minutes.

Serves 4

(Shrimp gumbo)

Prawns
in a light tomato sauce

28	large fresh prawns, heads and shells intact
1/3 cup	olive oil
4 tbsp	flour
3	large leeks, white and light green ends, minced
10	large garlic cloves, minced
1 bunch	fresh parsley, minced
1 tbsp	tomato paste
1 can	(28 oz) plum tomatoes, drained and puréed
1 cup	clam nectar or juice
10 oz	cold water
2 tbsp	white vinegar
1 tbsp	ground black pepper (or to taste)
1 tsp	salt

With a sharp pair of scissors, cut the legs and snouts off the prawns and discard. Rinse the bodies in cold water.

Heat the olive oil in a heavy-bottomed pot. Stir in the flour and sauté over a medium heat for about 12 minutes, creating a mahogany roux. Add the leeks, garlic and parsley and sauté until the leeks become limp. Blend in the tomato paste. Add the tomato purée, clam nectar or juice, water, vinegar, pepper and salt. Stir the ingredients well and simmer for 45 minutes.

Gently fold the prawns into the sauce and simmer for 8 to 12 minutes. Transfer to a shallow serving bowl.

Serves 4

During my commercial fishing years, we would drop prawn traps on the weekend and pick them up before heading home with our share. My dad would prepare this dish, one of the family's favourites.

If you prefer not to serve whole prawns, remove the heads and shells. Discard the shells but add the heads to the sauce while it is simmering. Discard them before adding the prawns. Serve with cooked cornmeal (see page 130), orzo or rice.

Eggplant STUFFED
with shrimp, crab and peppers

Prsut is a cured and air-dried ham similar to tasso and prosciutto, which can substitute for it. The eggplants may be stuffed earlier in the day, or even the night before, and kept under refrigeration. Bring them to room temperature before baking as directed.

2 medium	eggplants
½ lb	hand-peeled shrimp meat
½ lb	crab meat
4 slices	bacon, chopped
1 tbsp	butter
1	medium white onion, chopped
⅓ cup	minced fresh parsley
½ cup	chopped red bell pepper
¼ cup	minced green onions
½ tsp	coriander powder
½ tsp	thyme powder
½ tsp	salt
1 cup	bread chunks, soaked in milk
3	large eggs, lightly beaten
2 tbsp	thinly sliced and minced prsut
½ cup	fine bread crumbs
2 tbsp	olive oil

Preheat oven to 350°F.

To cook the eggplants, make a slit in the top, place on a rack over water and steam for 35 minutes or until tender. Cut in half lengthwise and remove the pulp from the centre, leaving approximately half an inch of flesh next to the skin.

Fry the bacon in a large frying pan. When it just begins to turn crisp, stir in the butter, onion, parsley, bell pepper and green onion. Sauté until the onion gets soft. Stir in the coriander, thyme and salt. Sauté for 3 to 5 minutes more. Transfer to a large bowl, add the eggs, bread chunks and the eggplant pulp, blending all the ingredients well. Gently fold in the shrimp and crab meat. Fill the eggplant halves with this mixture and place in a baking dish. Distribute the bread crumbs and prsut on top of each eggplant. Drizzle with olive oil and bake for 30 to 45 minutes.

Serves 4

Chicken baked with blood oranges (p 112)

Oysters hickory-seasoned and deep-fried (p 89)

Rižot od ligni

(Squid in rice with mushrooms and carrots)

1 lb	cleaned squid bodies
2 cups	arborio rice
1/4 cup	olive oil
1	large leek, white end only, minced
3	large garlic cloves, minced
1 cup	minced mushrooms
1/2 cup	grated carrots
1/2 tsp	ground black pepper
1/4 tsp	salt
1/8 tsp	dried and crushed red chilies
5 cups	chicken broth
2 tbsp	fresh lime juice
1/4 cup	minced fresh parsley

This is a Dalmatian dish that only my dad cooked. He made it at home and also on the boat when we were fishing. Like risotto, this requires frequent additions of broth to the rice and frequent stirring. While most risotto recipes call for simmering broth, I don't find that necessary.

Cut the squid bodies into 1/4-inch rings. Cut the heads in half.

Heat the olive oil in a large pot. Sauté the leeks, garlic, mushrooms and carrots until very tender, approximately 10 minutes. Stir in the pepper, salt and red chilies and sauté for another minute or so. Add the rice to the pot, blending it well with the vegetables.

Add 3/4 cup of chicken broth, stir and simmer until all the liquid is absorbed. Continue to add broth, 1/2 cup at a time, waiting until each addition has been absorbed before adding more. Cook and stir until the rice is tender. With the last addition of broth, stir in the squid. The entire cooking time will be 30 to 40 minutes. Add the lime juice and sprinkle with parsley.

Serves 4

SQUID
in a tomato clam-nectar sauce

One of my dad's first-pick dinners when served with cooked cornmeal (page 130), rice or orzo. Squid can be fairly big and tough, and while the small ones cost more, this recipe is best when made with small, tender squid. Prosciutto can replace the prsut.

2 lbs	small squid, cleaned, cut into ¾-inch rings
8 tbsp	olive oil, divided
2	onions, diced
8	very thin slices of prsut, chopped
2 tbsp	ground black pepper (or to taste)
½ cup	minced fresh parsley
1 tsp	coriander powder
1 tsp	paprika
1 tbsp	tomato paste
8	large plum tomatoes, peeled, seeded and chopped
1 cup	clam nectar or juice
½ tsp	dried and crushed red chilies
8	large garlic cloves, coarsely chopped
	flour

Heat 3 tablespoons of olive oil in a pot. Sauté the onions until limp. Stir in the prsut, pepper, parsley, coriander and paprika and sauté for 3 minutes. Stir in the tomato paste, blending it well. Remove the pot from the heat and stir in the plum tomatoes.

In another saucepan, bring the clam nectar or juice to a boil and reduce it by half. Add this reduced liquid to the onion mixture and bring to a simmer. Stir in the red chilies and simmer for 10 minutes. If the sauce is too thick, add a little hot water.

Heat 5 tablespoons of olive oil in a large frying pan. Dust the squid in flour, sauté half the squid and half the garlic for about 3 minutes at medium to high heat. Remove with a slotted spoon to a bowl. Repeat with the remaining squid and garlic. Combine all the squid and garlic with the onion-tomato mixture in the frying pan. Gently stir in the clam-nectar sauce, cover and simmer for 10 minutes.

Serves 4

Lešćo (Red snapper oven-poached with vegetables)

2	whole red snappers (2 lbs each), heads removed, cleaned and scaled
10	large garlic cloves, crushed and then mashed to a pulp
1/2 cup	minced fresh parsley
2 tbsp	coarse sea salt
2 tbsp	cumin powder
1 tbsp	coriander powder
1 tsp	ground black pepper
1/3 cup	fresh lime juice
8	medium Yukon gold potatoes, peeled, cut into 2-inch cubes
1	large celery root, in 1-inch cubes
6	large carrots, in 2-inch lengths
4	medium leeks, white to green ends, in 3-inch lengths
1 cup	clam nectar or juice
3/4 cup	olive oil
	ground black pepper

The closest translation for lešćo *is poached or lightly boiled. Similar one-dish dinners can be found throughout Croatia, Portugal and Spain. The whole fish is brought to the table on a platter and served with vegetables and a heavy bread, such as sourdough.*

Preheat oven to 450°F.

Combine the garlic, parsley, salt, cumin powder, coriander powder, pepper and lime juice in a bowl. Rub the spice mixture all over the fish, inside and out, and put them into a baking dish. Cover with plastic food wrap and refrigerate for 1 hour.

Remove the fish from the refrigerator and spread the potatoes, celery root, carrots and leeks around them in the baking dish. Pour the clam nectar or juice and olive oil over top of the fish and vegetables. Sprinkle with pepper and bake for 40 minutes. Baste several times during the baking period.

Arrange the snapper and vegetables on a large serving platter and ladle the broth into a gravy boat.

Serves 4

Riba marinada
(marinated halibut)

In my dad's home town of Crkvenica, this dish was prepared with a mackerel-type fish. My mother usually used halibut or in some cases replaced the halibut with smelts. Serve at room temperature along with some boiled potatoes, steamed vegetables and a tomato salad.

Marinada can be kept in the refrigerator for up to two weeks. It improves with age, and so I like to keep half to serve at a later meal.

6	halibut steaks (8 oz each), ¾-inch thick
4 tbsp	olive oil
	flour
8	large onions, sliced very thin
6	large garlic cloves, minced
1 bunch	fresh parsley, minced
1½ tbsp	ground black pepper
½ tsp	marjoram powder
½ tsp	coriander powder
¼ tsp	minced fresh dill
¼ cup	olive oil
	white vinegar
	cold water

Heat the olive oil in a large frying pan. Dredge the halibut in the flour and fry 3 to 4 minutes a side until the steaks are lightly browned. Remove and place on a large platter. Sauté the onions in the same pan until limp. Stir in the garlic, parsley, pepper, marjoram, coriander and dill, sautéing for 3 minutes. Transfer to a bowl and set aside.

Remove the bones from the halibut steaks. Doing this will divide each steak into 4 sections. Be careful not to break the fish into smaller pieces.

Put layers of fish and the onion mixture in a large glass bowl, finishing with a layer of the onion mixture.

Make enough marinade to cover the fish by combining 2 parts cold water to 1 part vinegar in a blender. Add the olive oil and blend well. (Start with 1 cup water to ½ cup vinegar and make more if necessary but don't add more oil.) Ladle the marinade over the fish. Cover with plastic food wrap and refrigerate overnight.

Serves 4 (at two sittings)

Beef stew with chard (and kale)

2 lb	top round beef roast, cut into 2-inch cubes
1 bunch	Swiss chard, washed and chopped
1 bunch	kale, washed and chopped
1/4 cup	olive oil
2	large white onions, chopped
6	garlic cloves, minced
1 tbsp	grated fresh ginger
1 tsp	thyme powder
1 tsp	coriander powder
1/2 tsp	salt
1/2 tsp	dried and crushed red chilies
6	large plum tomatoes, peeled, seeded and chopped
4–5 cups	beef broth

The carrots and potatoes of your average stew are missing from this one. In their place are the greens and the surprising flavour of ginger. It makes a great meal for a large family or you can freeze half for later. A loaf of good, chewy bread is a must with this meal.

Place the Swiss chard and kale in a stock pot, cover with water, add 1 tablespoon of salt and simmer for 10 minutes. Drain well, place in a glass bowl and set aside.

Heat the oil in a large pot. Sauté the meat and onions on medium to high heat until browned. Add the garlic, ginger, thyme, coriander, salt, red chilies and tomatoes and sauté for 5 minutes. Cover these ingredients with beef broth. Put a lid on the pot and simmer on low to medium heat for 30 to 45 minutes or until the meat is tender. Stir several times.

Remove the stew from the heat and stir in the Swiss chard and kale, replace the lid and allow to stand for 5 minutes just to heat the vegetables.

Serves 6 to 8

polpeta

If you do not have the time to make the béchamel sauce, replace it with a can (10 oz) of cream of mushroom soup whisked with three quarters of a can (7 ½ oz) undiluted chicken broth.

½ lb bacon, finely chopped
¾ lb lean ground pork
½ lb ground veal
½ lb lean ground beef
2 green onion bunches, minced
2 tsp ground black pepper (or to taste)
2 large eggs
¾ lb mushrooms, halved
4 garlic cloves, minced
¼ cup water
2 cups béchamel sauce (see page 151)

Preheat oven to 325°F.

Sauté the bacon in a large frying pan until crisp. Remove with a slotted spoon and set aside.

Combine the pork, veal, beef, bacon and the green onion in a large bowl. Add the pepper and eggs and blend well. Shape the meat into 12 patties, ½ inch to ¾ inch thick. Fry the patties in the bacon drippings. When they are well done, put them in a baking dish.

Drain the bacon fat from the pan without removing any browned meat particles. Sauté the mushrooms for 5 minutes. Stir in the garlic and water and simmer for 5 minutes, making sure to pick up all the browned meat particles. Add the béchamel sauce to the frying pan and bring to a low simmer for 5 minutes. Pour the sauce over the meat patties, cover and bake for 30 minutes.

Serves 4 to 6

(meat patties in mushroom sauce)

Romaine salad with kefalotir cheese

½ head	romaine lettuce, washed, torn into bite-size pieces
6	large mushrooms, sliced thin
2	plum tomatoes, cut into wedges
½	small English cucumber, seeded and cut into chunks
1	small red onion, sliced very thin
16	kalamata olives
2	large limes, juiced
¼ cup	olive oil
2 tbsp	white vinegar
1 tsp	balsamic vinegar
1 tsp	ground black pepper
¼ tsp	salt
¼ cup	grated kefalotir cheese
4	anchovies, quartered

This combination of the lime-juice-flavoured vegetables with the olive oil and vinegar dressing is refreshing. Kefalotir is a hard cheese that can be grated; Parmesan is an acceptable substitute.

Place the romaine in a bowl, cover with plastic food wrap and refrigerate. Combine the mushrooms, tomatoes, cucumbers, onions and olives in a bowl. Squeeze the lime juice over and toss.

Prepare a dressing by whisking the olive oil, vinegars, pepper and salt in a bowl. Add half of this mixture to the vegetables and toss lightly.

Arrange the romaine on a deep-dished serving platter. Spoon the vegetable mixture over top. Sprinkle on the cheese and anchovies. Drizzle the remaining dressing over the salad.

Serves 4

Omelette with ASPARAGUS and TOMATO OLIVE SALSA

This has been a Sunday brunch favourite in my own home for years, so much so that our weekend guests request it. The Tomato Olive Salsa may be prepared the day before and warmed when ready to serve.

1 cup	Tomato Olive Salsa (see p 153)
6	large eggs
2 tbsp	ice-cold water
1/2 tsp	ground black pepper
1/4 tsp	salt
3 tbsp	butter
1/2 cup	fresh, slender asparagus, in 1/2-inch pieces
1/2 cup	bacon, fried crisp and crumbled
1/2 cup	coarsely grated sharp Cheddar cheese
1/4 cup	green onions, in 1/2-inch pieces

Prepare the Tomato Olive Salsa in a saucepan and keep warm on the stove.

Beat the eggs in a bowl. Add the water, pepper and salt and beat until blended.

Heat 1 tablespoon of butter in a large, nonstick frying pan. Sauté the asparagus, bacon and green onion until warmed and the vegetables just begin to soften. Remove to a bowl and set aside.

Melt the remaining 2 tablespoons of butter in the frying pan. Pour the egg mixture into the pan. When the edges begin to set, sprinkle the asparagus, bacon, cheese and green onion evenly over half the omelette's surface. When the omelette is set but the top is still moist, take two wide spatulas and flip the unadorned half over onto the vegetable-covered half. Cover and cook for 2 minutes.

Slide the omelette out of the pan onto a large serving platter. Spoon the Tomato Olive Salsa, lengthwise over the centre and serve immediately.

Serves 4

FIREHALL FAVOURITES

The recipes in this book are ones I've cooked for family and friends, which doesn't exclude the firefighters I work with in the Vancouver Fire and Rescue Service. Many firefighters are my friends, and those I crew with in a firehall are more like family. We work together on ten- and fourteen-hour shifts. We cook for each other and we sit down together to eat the same meal. We even sleep in the same bedroom. And when we've returned to the hall after a tough fire, we sometimes share our fears, just like family.

When I came into the service 31 years ago, firehall cooking was cheap and quick. The guys liked to cook in bulk. They had a meal they called "slag" which was just a huge batch of macaroni and cheese. Coming from a family that really cared about food, I wasn't about to spend the rest of my working life eating that stuff. When it was my turn to cook, I began to elevate the culinary level, introducing such things as crab, steamed clams and more fruit and vegetables.

We all chip in to buy the ingredients for our meals, and I got the reputation of being an expensive cook. If the other guys' meals cost a buck, mine cost two. Eventually I became the special occasion chef – for birthdays, retirements and promotions.

As in any family, my firefighting buddies got to know and love some of my more practical dishes, and those are the ones I've chosen for this chapter.

oven-baked, European-style salami

2 lbs	lean ground beef
2 lbs	lean ground pork
4	large garlic cloves, minced
3 tbsp	ground black black pepper
2 tbsp	paprika
2 tbsp	granulated onion
2 tbsp	coriander
2 tbsp	mustard seed
1 tbsp	pickling spice

Combine all the ingredients in a bowl and blend well. Shape the meat into 3 logs about 8 inches long. Wrap tightly in a few layers of cheesecloth and tie the ends tightly with cotton twine. Refrigerate overnight.

Preheat the oven to 200 to 225°F. Place the logs directly on the middle oven rack with a pan on the lower rack to catch any drippings. Cook for 6 to 8 hours. When done to your preference, place the logs on a cookie rack and allow to cool. Remove the cheesecloth before slicing.

Yields 3 logs

We used to make a huge batch of these logs in the firehall in December. The whole crew would be involved, and everyone would take some home to have on hand for holiday guests.

The logs will be cooked in five hours. Over the next three hours, they will become drier. To discover how dry you prefer the salami to be, you could remove one of the three logs from the oven after six, seven and finally eight hours. The logs will keep for four to six weeks under refrigeration.

CORNED BEEF with an orange-lemon crust

Firefighters loved this recipe which I found in Fredericksburg, Texas. I just took out the original's over-powering cayenne and chili peppers and used mustard powder for zing.

Always rinse off the spices in which the brisket was cured. Do not cook potatoes and cabbage in the water with the meat because everything will taste the same. With a pressure cooker, the cooking time will be about two hours. Without a pressure cooker, allow four hours.

1	corned beef brisket (3 lbs)
1/2 cup	brown sugar
2 tbsp	fine bread crumbs
1 tbsp	mustard powder
1	large orange
1	large lemon
1/4 cup	apple cider, hard or soft

Preheat oven to 300° F.

Rinse the brisket under cold water to remove any spices. Place in a pressure cooker, cover with water and bring to a boil. Pressure cook for 1 hour or until the meat is tender. If you do not have a pressure cooker, cover the meat with water and simmer for an hour a pound.

Grate and juice the orange and lemon, reserving the juices and zests separately. Combine the brown sugar, bread crumbs, and orange and lemon zests.

Drain the meat and place in a baking dish. Spread the brown sugar mixture over top, patting it on well. Combine the orange and lemon juices with the apple cider and gently baste the meat several times while it bakes for about 45 minutes.

Place on a serving dish and slice across the grain.

Serves 4

Hank's Dutch-Indonesian nasi goring

1	3-lb round roast of beef
1 cup	white rice
2 pkgs	nasi goring mix (5 oz each)
6	large eggs
1	large onion
4	large garlic cloves
2 tbsp	olive oil, divided
2 tbsp	sambal oelek
½ lb	fresh shrimp meat
1 tbsp	black pepper
1 tsp	salt

Day One

Preheat oven to 350° F.

To roast the beef, rub about 1 tablespoon of oil on the bottom of a roasting pan. Put the roast in the pan (I don't use a rack) and roast until well done. Cool to room temperature, dice the meat into ½-inch cubes, wrap and store in the refrigerator.

Drain the oil from the roasting pan, making sure to save all the meat juices and browned particles. Add a little water to the pan, place on low to medium heat and simmer, scraping up all the browned bits off the bottom of the pan. Add the nasi goring mix, and cook until the mix softens, approximately 10 minutes. You may have to add a little more water. Transfer to a bowl, cover and refrigerate.

Cook the rice. When it is cool, transfer to a bowl, cover and refrigerate.

Beat the eggs. Add 2 tablespoons of cold water and beat again. Make 6 to 8 egg crêpes by frying the beaten egg in small amounts at a time in a nonstick frying pan, as you would for thin crêpes. When they are cool, cut the crêpes into ½-inch strips, wrap in plastic food wrap and refrigerate.

Hank is a retired firefighter who gave me this recipe. I've cooked it in the firehalls of Vancouver for many years, and it's always a hit.

Although the recipe seems difficult, it is made easier by dividing the work over two days. Roast the beef and make the rice and egg crêpes the day before. Allow one to two hours the next day for the final baking.

Sambal oelek, a commercial hot pepper sauce, is readily available, as is the nasi goring spice mix.

Day Two

Finally chop the shrimp and the onion and mince the garlic. Heat the olive oil in a large frying pan. Sauté the onion and garlic until the onions turn light brown. Stir in the sambal oelek and add the diced meat, stirring often. When the meat is heated, stir in the nasi goring mixture and the chopped shrimp meat and cook for 5 to 10 minutes. You may have to add a little water to prevent sticking.

Remove the mixture from the heat and allow to cool. Divide the mixture in half and combine each half with half the rice. Re-combine everything in one roasting pan. Stir in the strips of egg crêpes, toss well and set aside until ready to cook.

Heat oven to 350°F. Place the uncovered roasting pan in the oven and bake until the meat mixture just begins to lose all its moisture. Toss and stir several times. This will take 1 to 2 hours.

Serve with a purchased sweet soy sauce or chutney and with sliced cucumbers and bananas.

Serves 6 to 8

east end roast

¾ lb	ground veal
½ lb	lean ground beef
½ lb	very lean ground pork
½ lb	bacon slices
½ cup	chopped green onion
¼ cup	minced celery heart (the tender, inner ribs)
2	garlic cloves, minced
1 cup	crushed salted crackers
½ cup	chopped fresh parsley
1	large egg
¼ cup	chili sauce
1 tbsp	mustard powder
1 tbsp	Worcestershire sauce
1 tsp	ground black pepper
½ tsp	salt
1 tbsp	olive oil

Many years ago meatloaf was given this nickname in the firehalls of working-class Vancouver. The chili sauce and mustard in my recipe lift it above the "roast" that was common when I began my career with the fire department. Because this meatloaf isn't cooked in a loaf pan but in an open dish, it gets nicely browned all over.

Preheat oven to 350°F.

Chop the bacon and fry until crisp. Put the veal, beef, pork and fried bacon in a large bowl and mix gently to combine. Add the green onion, celery, garlic, crackers and parsley, again combining gently. Add the egg, chili sauce, mustard powder, Worcestershire sauce, pepper and salt, mixing until combined.

Oil the bottom of a baking dish, shape the meat mixture into a loaf and place in the centre of the baking dish. Roast for about 1 hour or until an instant-read thermometer reaches 165°F.

Allow the roast to stand for 10 minutes before slicing.

Serves 4

Curried **veal shanks** in a pot

Curry dishes have always been a favourite in Vancouver firehalls, and I have been asked to cook this one over and over again. I serve it with fried rice and steamed cauliflower.

Check out my comments on curry powder (page 44).

4	veal shanks (2 inches thick)
1/2 cup	flour
1/4 cup	curry powder
2 tbsp	coriander powder
3 tbsp	olive oil
3 tbsp	butter
2	medium white onions, halved and sliced very thin
4	large garlic cloves, minced
1/2 tsp	salt
2 cups	port wine
2 cups	vegetable broth
	ground black pepper

Tie the shanks with butcher's twine to keep the meat from falling off the bone.

Combine the flour, curry powder and coriander powder in a shallow bowl, blending them well.

Heat the olive oil and butter in a large, heavy pot. Dredge the veal shanks in the flour mixture and fry in the oil and butter until well browned on both sides. Remove to a platter and set aside. Hold the leftover flour-spice mixture.

Add the onion to the pot and sauté until well browned. This will take up to 30 minutes. Stir in the garlic and salt and sauté for 5 minutes. Stir in about 2 tablespoons of the remaining flour-spice mixture to make a light roux, stirring until it turns to a tan colour. Gradually stir in the port wine and bring to a boil.

Put the veal shanks in a single layer in the pot and add the vegetable broth. Cover and simmer for 1 1/2 to 2 hours until the meat is very tender.

Remove the lid and simmer for 20 to 30 minutes until the sauce thickens and will cling to a spoon.

Remove the shanks with tongs, cut away the butcher's twine and place one on each of 4 dinner plates. Spoon equal amounts of onion and sauce over top and sprinkle with pepper. Serves 4

Chicken and garlic with wine and mushrooms

2	chicken breasts, skinned and split
4	chicken legs, skinned
4	chicken thighs, skinned
	flour
3 tbsp	olive oil
2 tbsp	ground black pepper (or to taste)
1 1/2 lbs	mushrooms, halved
1 cup	minced celery hearts (the tender, innner ribs)
10	large garlic cloves, slivered lengthwise
1 bottle	(10 oz) red cooking wine (e.g., Tosca)

Preheat oven to 350°F.

Heat the olive oil in a medium frying pan. Dredge the chicken pieces in flour and brown well in the olive oil. Sprinkle the bottom of a baking dish with the pepper. When all the chicken pieces are fried, put them in a single layer on top of the pepper.

Add the mushrooms and celery to the frying pan and sauté for 5 minutes. Stir in the garlic, add the cooking wine and bring to a low simmer for 3 to 5 minutes, making sure that all the browned bits have been scraped up off the bottom of the pan. Pour the sauce over the chicken, cover and bake for 45 minutes.

Serves 4

I designed this one at least twenty-five years ago, and it became a favourite with my crew. Now young fellows who have learned this recipe in other fire-halls attempt to impress me by cooking it for me.

The cooking wine I use is a seasoned product sold in grocery stores. It makes salt unnecessary. As for the pepper, there's no mistake – two tablespoons is the amount I like.

Cook some wild rice to serve with the chicken.

Cornish game hens SPICED
and roasted

Most people are used to having Cornish game hens stuffed with wild rice. This recipe was created in the firehall when I was trying to do something out of the ordinary with game hens.

After you have brushed the spice paste on the hens, you may cook them that day or 24 hours later.

2	large Cornish game hens, halved
4 tbsp	chili powder
2 tbsp	mustard flour
1 tbsp	ground black pepper
1 tbsp	dried and crushed red chilies
1 tsp	coriander powder
1 tsp	celery salt
	olive oil
4	large garlic cloves, minced
2 tbsp	olive oil

Put the chili powder, mustard flour, pepper, red chilies, coriander and celery salt in a bowl and mix well. Stir in just enough olive oil to create a thin paste. Add the garlic and blend well.

Brush this paste on the skin and underside of the cut hens using it all. Place in a dish, cover with plastic food wrap and refrigerate for 2 to 3 hours or up to 24 hours.

When you are ready to roast the hens, heat oven to 350°F.

Coat the bottom of a shallow roasting pan with olive oil. Put the hens, skin side up in the pan. Tent with aluminum foil and bake for 40 minutes.

Remove the foil, raise the heat to 400°F and roast the hens for 30 to 45 minutes more. The skin should be crisp and well browned. Place the hens on individual dinner plates and drizzle any juices from the pan over each one before serving.

Serves 4

Sea BASS

with papaya, cantaloupe and pimientos

2 lbs	sea bass fillets
	salt
1 tsp	ground black pepper
1 tbsp	olive oil
1/2 cup	undiluted frozen orange juice
1/3 cup	water
1	large papaya, peeled, seeded and diced
1/2	cantaloupe, peeled, seeded and diced
1/4 cup	pimientos, chopped
2 tbsp	minced fresh parsley
2 tbsp	sweet hot sauce (e.g., Tiger Sauce)
1 tsp	brown sugar

I once worked in a firehall with only three other firefighters. They were on a health kick, eating a lot of vegetables, fruit, chicken and fish. I usually fried or baked sea bass, but to please them I thought of adding fruit. Cod or red snapper also work well in this treatment.

Preheat oven to 375°F.

Cover the bottom of a shallow roasting pan with the olive oil. Arrange the fillets in the pan and sprinkle with the pepper and a little salt.

Prepare an orange glaze by simmering the orange juice and water in a small saucepan until the liquid boils away to a thick syrup.

Prepare the fruit sauce by combining the papaya, cantaloupe, pimientos, parsley, sweet hot sauce and brown sugar in a medium frying pan. Cook over medium heat. When the ingredients are heated, cover and set aside.

Bake the fish for 10 to 12 minutes. Raise the oven temperature to 425°F and bake for 8 minutes more, basting with the orange glaze until it is all used.

Arrange the fillets on a serving platter. Bring the fruit sauce to a quick bubble and spoon over the fish.

Serves 4

White pasta sauce with garlic

On a busy day in the firehall, we would cook this easy pasta sauce because we could have dinner ready in about 30 minutes. We usually served it with grilled sausages and a green salad.

½ lb	butter
1 cup	freshly grated Parmesan
½ cup	whipping cream
6	large garlic cloves, minced
½ tbsp	ground black pepper
2	egg yolks
¾ lb	pasta
¼ cup	minced fresh parsley

Prepare a sauce by melting the butter in a medium saucepan. Remove from the heat and stir in the Parmesan. Add the whipping cream, garlic and pepper. Whisk in the egg yolks, blending all the ingredients well.

Cook the pasta. Drain and return to the pot on very low heat. Bring the sauce to a boil. If the sauce is too thick, add a touch of hot water. Immediately toss the pasta with the sauce. Transfer the pasta to a large serving bowl and sprinkle with parsley.

Serves 4

BRUSSELS SPROUTS with
balsamic vinaigrette

20	Brussels sprouts, trimmed and halved length-wise
1/4 cup	olive oil
1 tbsp	vinegar
1/2 tsp	balsamic vinegar
2	medium garlic cloves, minced
1 tbsp	ground black pepper (or to taste)
1/2 tsp	salt

Steam the Brussels sprouts for 10 minutes.

Prepare the dressing by combining the olive oil, vinegars, garlic, pepper and salt in a small jar. Put a lid on the jar and shake well. When the Brussels sprouts are cooked, put them in a serving bowl. Drizzle the dressing over top and toss gently.

Serves 4

For years many fire-fighters told me that they didn't like "those little cabbages." I prepared them the way my mother used to and, lo and behold, they were asking for the recipe.

Potato pancakes WITH
YUKON GOLDS

*When I first intro-
duced this to the fire-
hall, all the guys
went crazy over
them. Yukon golds
are best for this
recipe because they
remain firm enough
to grate even when
cooked.*

*Since most of us do
not save chicken fat,
you may substitute
bacon drippings or
olive oil. I buy apple
butter to serve with
the pancakes.*

6	large unpeeled Yukon gold potatoes
3	large eggs, well beaten
2 tbsp	fine crumbs made from salted crackers
1 tbsp	flour
4 tbsp	chicken fat

Cook the potatoes. When they are cool, peel and grate
them. Add the eggs, crackers and flour, mixing well with
your fingers.

Heat the chicken fat in a medium frying pan. Put the
potato mixture into the frying pan ¼ cup at a time and flatten out to produce small pancakes. Brown slowly over low
to medium heat, about 4 minutes a side, until the edges
become crisp.

Serves 4

SPICY HOT DISHES

I have a liking for spicy food, which may be inherited. Croatian dishes are fairly peppery. In travelling around the American south, I've eaten in restaurants in Louisiana, Texas, New Mexico and Florida, trying out Creole and Cajun cooking. Most of the recipes in this chapter are re-creations of dishes I've eaten there.

If there's fire in your mouth when you eat these dishes, blame the capsaicinoids – heat-producing chemicals in peppers. These chemicals are measured in Scoville heat units: bell peppers have none; habaneros, the hottest, have from 200,000 to 300,000. The dried red chilies I often use come from cayenne peppers, with a Scoville rating of 35,000 to 60,000.

The chili powders sold in most supermarkets are blends of ground chilies, other spices and salt. Chances are they have not been carefully handled during shipping and will have lost a percentage of their taste, aroma and heat. A brand I can recommend is Gebhardt. I buy it in five-pound bottles whenever I'm in the U.S. and keep it in my freezer. The same shipping problems can bedevil curry powder, and so I order mine from Pendery's Inc. (Addresses for both products are on page 159.)

If you catch fire while eating these dishes, the best fire extinguishers are bread, rice, avocado (why do you think guacamole was invented?) or milk. Don't bother with water.

Be careful when handling peppers, especially the ribs and seeds. Wear gloves or wash your hands after.

FETTUCINI WITH HOT SAUSAGE AND SPINACH

1 lb	hot Italian sausages, casings removed
2 tbsp	olive oil
1	medium white onion, minced
2 cups	chopped celery leaves
4	large garlic cloves, minced
1 can	(5 ½ oz) tomato paste
2 cups	chicken broth
1 tbsp	whole dried Mexican oregano
1 tsp	ground black pepper
1 lb	fettucini
1 bunch	fresh spinach, washed, drained and chopped
⅓ cup	freshly grated Parmesan

I created this recipe when I worked in a west-end Vancouver firehall where the crew was really into spicy-hot foods. Let me warn you: this is hot. To moderate the fire, try a combination of a half pound hot sausage with a half pound of mild. That should cut the heat by a third.

Fry the sausage meat in a medium frying pan until well browned, breaking it into small pieces as it cooks. Remove the meat with a slotted spoon and set aside. Discard the fat but reserve all the browned meat particles.

Sauté the olive oil, onion, celery leaves and garlic in the frying pan until the onions are limp, scraping all the browned bits off the bottom of the pan. Blend in the tomato paste. Add the chicken broth. Crush the oregano between your fingers and add to the frying pan along with the pepper.

Return the sausage meat to the pan, cover and simmer for 1 hour. If the sauce becomes too thick, add a little water.

Cook the pasta. Drain well and return to the pot, add the spinach, cover and allow to stand for 2 minutes. Transfer the pasta and spinach to a serving bowl, ladle the sauce over top and sprinkle with the Parmesan.

Serves 4

cabbage rolls

Another creation from Cajun country, although I have replaced the local sausage with a hot Italian sausage. It's worth hunting for jamon serrano, which Saveur *magazine calls Europe's highest-quality cured and dried ham, but prsut or prosciutto are good substitutes.*

Steaming the cabbage to make the leaves tender for rolling may take as long as 45 minutes, with the final stovetop cooking taking another 45 minutes.

1 ½ lbs	hot Italian sausage meat
1 tbsp	olive oil
1	medium white onion, minced
¼ cup	very thinly sliced and chopped jamon serrano, prosciutto or prsut
¾ cup	minced green cabbage
2	medium garlic cloves, minced
2	large plum tomatoes, skinned and chopped
3 tbsp	minced fresh parsley
½ tsp	thyme powder
¼ tsp	cayenne pepper
1	large bay leaf
2	large eggs
1	large Savoy cabbage
	yogurt or sour cream

To prepare the cabbage leaves, core the cabbage, which will hasten the cooking. Put 2 inches of water into a large pot and set the cabbage upright in the pot. Bring the water to a rolling simmer and cover the pot. Steam for about 30 to 45 minutes. Put the cabbage into a large quantity of cold water (I fill my kitchen sink) and remove any leaves that are tender and pull away easily. Return the cabbage to the pot and continue to steam until the inner leaves are tender, which will happen very quickly.

Heat the olive oil in a medium frying pan. Add the onion and sauté until lightly browned. Sauté the sausage meat, breaking it into small pieces. Cook until the meat is well done. Add the jamon serrano, minced green cabbage and garlic and cook until the cabbage becomes limp. Stir in the tomatoes, parsley, thyme, cayenne and bay leaf. Cook for about 10 minutes or until the mixture thickens and there is no liquid left in the pan.

Remove the bay leaf and allow the mixture to cool. Add the eggs and using your hands, blend all the ingredients well.

creole-style

To make the cabbage rolls, slice the heavy white vein off each leaf. Place about 1/4 cup of the meat mixture on a cabbage leaf. From the bottom, roll the leaf half way. Fold in the sides and continue rolling. Place the rolls seam-side down in a single layer in a large frying pan. Add 3 to 4 tablespoons of water, cover and simmer for 30 to 45 minutes until the cabbage is very tender. Serve with yogurt or sour cream.

Serves 4

Chicken casserole

with eggplant, roasted bell peppers and okra

For drama, I like to present this one-dish dinner from the south-western U.S. in a clear glass casserole so that the attractive colours of the green beans, tomatoes and red peppers are displayed.

Some people serve this with refried beans; I usually choose rice.

Don't underestimate the heat of the red chilies.

12	large boneless chicken breast halves, skinned
4 tbsp	olive oil, divided
1	large white onion, finely chopped
1	medium eggplant, peeled, cut into 2-inch cubes
1/2 lb	string beans, in 2-inch pieces
6	plum tomatoes, peeled, seeded, cut into 1/2-inch slices
1 cup	coarsely chopped roasted red bell peppers (see page 152)
1/2 lb	fresh okra, topped and tipped, cut into 1/8-inch slices
2 tbsp	chicken bouillon granules
1 1/2 tbsp	dried and crushed red chilies
1/2 tbsp	ground black pepper
1/2 tbsp	cumin powder

Preheat oven to 350°F.

Heat 2 tablespoons of the olive oil in a medium frying pan and sauté the chicken in batches until browned. Remove with a slotted spoon and set aside. Add the remaining 2 tablespoons of olive oil to the frying pan and sauté the onion, eggplant and string beans for 3 to 5 minutes. Remove to a large bowl. Add the tomatoes, red peppers and okra to the bowl and toss gently.

Place 4 pieces of chicken on the bottom of a glass casserole and sprinkle with about a third of the chicken bouillon granules, red chilies, pepper and cumin. Spread a third of the vegetable mixture over the chicken. Make three layers of chicken and vegetables, sprinkling each layer of chicken with the seasonings. Pour the oil and browned particles from the frying pan over the top layer. Cover and bake for 30 minutes. Remove the lid and bake for 10 minutes more.

Serves 4 to 6

SOUTHERN

1	chicken (3 lbs), cut into 10 pieces
5 tbsp	olive oil
¼ cup	curry powder
6	cloves garlic, minced
1 tbsp	finely grated fresh ginger
1 tsp	dried and crushed red chilies
1 tsp	turmeric powder
1 tsp	ground black pepper
	cold water
1	large onion, chopped
2 tbsp	tomato paste
1 ½ tsp	salt

Blend the curry powder, garlic, ginger, red chilies, turmeric and pepper in a small bowl. Add cold water a little at a time until you have a thick paste.

Heat the olive oil in a deep, medium frying pan. Sauté the chicken pieces in batches until golden brown. Remove and set aside.

Sauté the onions in the frying pan until lightly browned. Stir in the salt, curry paste and tomato paste.

Return the chicken pieces to the frying pan and add just enough hot water to almost cover them. Cover the pan and simmer on low heat for 30 to 45 minutes.

Serves 4

Years ago most fire-fighters made a curry sauce with cream of mushroom soup as the base. I always joked that Campbell's must send tankers of the stuff to India. I still avoid curry dishes that are soupy or in a white sauce.

CHICKEN

CURRY

picadillo
with olives, raisins and capers

With some substitutions for hard-to-find ingredients, this recipe is one that came from Armando's, a small bar in Havana. Don't make the picadillo runny; you are not cooking up a pot of chili!

2 lbs	coarsely ground lean pork
1 lb	coarsely ground veal
3 tbsp	olive oil
1	large onion, chopped
1	red bell pepper, chopped
1	large leek, white end only, minced
3	large garlic cloves, minced
4 tbsp	chili powder
1 tbsp	ground black pepper
1/2 tsp	cumin powder
1 tsp	dried and crushed red chilies
1 can	(28 oz) plum tomatoes, drained and chopped
1/2 cup	chopped pitted black olives
1/4 cup	golden raisins, softened in water and drained
1 tbsp	capers
1 can	(15 oz) black beans, drained

Heat the olive oil in a deep, medium frying pan. Add the onion, bell pepper and leeks and sauté until limp. Stir in the garlic and sauté for 5 minutes.

Add the pork and veal and sauté until the meat is well browned. Stir in the chili powder, pepper, cumin, red chilies and chopped tomatoes and simmer for 5 minutes.

Blend in the olives, raisins and capers. Cover and simmer for 20 minutes. If there is not enough liquid, add a little water. Fold in the black beans being careful not to crush them. Cover and simmer just long enough to heat the beans.

Serves 4 to 6

Beef fillet **steaks** in *mole* sauce

2	beef fillet steaks (6 oz each)
1 tsp	chili powder
1 tsp	ground black pepper
1/2 tsp	coriander powder
1/4 tsp	salt
3 tbsp	olive oil, divided
2	yellow bell peppers, cleaned and chopped
2	yellow peppers, "hots", cleaned and chopped
1	medium onion, chopped
4	large garlic cloves, chopped
1/2 tsp	cinnamon powder
1/2 tsp	allspice powder
1/4 tsp	nutmeg powder
3	canned tomatillos, chopped
1 tbsp	sugar
1 tsp	salt
4	medium shallots, sliced

A steak with a Tex-Mex accent. Some mole *sauces contain chocolate, but those I ate in the southern U.S. did not.*

The peppers known as yellow hots are equal in heat to jalapeños.

Make this simple and delicious by serving it with boiled potatoes and a mixture of steamed spinach, Swiss chard and beet tops.

Combine the chili powder, pepper, coriander and salt. Rub the steaks with the spices. Cover with plastic food wrap and keep at room temperature.

Heat 2 tablespoons of the olive oil in a medium saucepan. Add the peppers, onion, garlic, cinnamon, allspice, nutmeg and tomatillos and sauté over medium heat for 10 to 15 minutes. Transfer to a food processor and purée. Strain into a nonstick saucepan. Stir in the sugar and salt, bring to a boil, lower the heat and simmer for 2 minutes. Cover and remove from the heat.

Heat the remaining 1 tablespoon of olive oil in a medium, heavy-bottomed frying pan. Sear the steaks on medium to high heat for 3 to 4 minutes a side. Put the steaks on individual dinner plates and keep warm. Sauté the shallots in the frying pan until limp, from 3 to 5 minutes.

Top the steaks with the shallots. Drizzle the *mole* sauce over the steaks and halfway around the outer edge of the dinner plates. Serves 2

white fish in
SPICY TOMATO SAUCE

I always choose sea bass for this recipe but the firmer white fishes, such as ocean perch or the faithful red snapper, are acceptable substitutes. I like to serve this with rice.

1 1/2 lbs	white fish, cut into 3-inch pieces
2 tbsp	olive oil
1	medium onion, halved and thinly sliced
5	large plum tomatoes, peeled, seeded and diced
1	large yellow bell pepper, minced
3	jalapeño peppers, stemmed, seeded and minced
2	large garlic cloves, minced
1/2 tsp	grated fresh ginger
1/2 tsp	ground black pepper
1/4 tsp	salt
1/4 tsp	cinnamon powder
1/4 cup	V8 Vegetable Cocktail

Heat the olive oil in a deep, medium frying pan. Sauté the onion, tomatoes, bell pepper, jalapeño pepper and garlic until limp. Stir in the ginger, pepper, salt and cinnamon powder and sauté for 3 minutes. Add the V8 juice and cook for 10 minutes, stirring often.

Add the fish to the frying pan. If there is not enough sauce, add just a little water or white wine. Cover and simmer for 8 to 12 minutes.

Serves 4

Sea bass with papaya, cantaloupe and pimientos (p 39)

Rock shrimp sauté with asparagus, corn and papaya (p 87)

Cajun prawns with **BANANAS** and rice

24	fresh prawns, heads removed, peeled, tails left on
1 tbsp	olive oil
1 ½ tbsp	butter
2 tbsp	flour
1	medium white onion, coarsely chopped
2 cups	chopped celery heart (the tender, inner ribs)
6	medium garlic cloves, minced
1	medium jalapeño, cleaned, seeded and minced
3 tbsp	fresh lime juice
1 tbsp	ground black pepper
1 tbsp	sugar
½ tsp	salt
6	large plum tomatoes, skinned and chopped
1–2 cups	chicken broth
2	large green bananas, in ½-inch slices
1 cup	white rice
2 tbsp	minced fresh parsley

In Corpus Christi, Texas, I had the opportunity to go out into the Gulf of Mexico on a shrimp boat for a 24-hour trip. The crew caught several sizes of shrimp. I saw that some of their shrimp were larger than our prawns and usually a lot sweeter. As a result, when I make a Cajun dish that calls for shrimp, I substitute prawns.

Cook the rice and keep it warm in a colander over simmering water.

Heat the oil and butter in a medium pot or large saucepan. Stir in the flour and sauté over medium heat until you have a brown roux.

Add the onion, celery and garlic. Sauté until the onion is tender. Stir in the jalapeño, lime juice, pepper, sugar, salt and tomatoes. Add just enough chicken broth to make a sauce with a fairly thick consistency. Bring the sauce to a simmer, add the prawns, cover and cook for 12 minutes.

Remove from the heat and stir in the banana. Replace the lid and allow to stand for 3 minutes, just to heat the banana.

Scoop the rice into the centre of a shallow serving bowl. Arrange the prawns around the outer edge, ladle the sauce over the rice and sprinkle with parsley.

Serves 4

Greens

IN A MUSTARD HOT SAUCE

*A traditional veg-
etable dish served in
many southern
states. The greens
change with the sea-
son. I sometimes use
spinach or beet tops,
and I really do put in
a tablespoon of
black pepper.*

1 bunch	kale, washed and trimmed
1 bunch	red chard, washed and trimmed
2 tbsp	butter
1 tbsp	ground black pepper (or to taste)
1/2 tsp	salt
1 tsp	mustard powder
3 tbsp	cold water
2 tbsp	butter, melted
1 tbsp	sweet hot sauce (e.g., Tiger Sauce)

Heat the butter in a deep frying pan large enough to hold
the bulky greens. Sauté the kale on medium to high heat
until it begins to wilt. Transfer to a non-metallic bowl and
set aside. Add the red chard to the frying pan and sauté for 3
minutes. Return the kale to the pan, add the pepper and
salt and toss well.

Blend the mustard and water together and add to the
pan. Cover and steam for 5 to 8 minutes. Remove the lid
and cook until all the liquid evaporates. Transfer the greens
to a serving bowl. Combine the melted butter and sweet
hot sauce, drizzle over the greens and toss.

Serves 4

Corn niblets panfried with roasted bell peppers

3 cups   corn niblets
1 tbsp   butter
1 tbsp   olive oil
⅓ cup   chopped roasted red bell peppers (see page 152)
¼ tsp   dried and crushed red chilies

Heat the butter and olive oil in a medium frying pan. Add the corn niblets, roasted bell peppers and chilies. Raise the heat to medium and sauté until the corn niblets begin to brown and get chewy. This may take anywhere from 10 to 20 minutes with regular stirring.

Serves 4

You could use frozen or canned corn niblets (two 12-ounce cans) or slice the niblets from five to six fresh or frozen cobs.

Since I began pan-frying corn niblets, I have never simply heated canned corn. This method is easy, but the results are much more interesting.

DINNER APPETIZERS

Escargots with PROVOLONE

I created this dish for my wife, Pat. To this day she would rather eat escargots at home than at any of the restaurants we frequent.

2 cans (24) snails, drained
½ cup olive oil
⅓ cup butter
8 large garlic cloves, minced
¼ cup minced white onion
1 tsp seafood seasoning (i.e., Old Bay Seasoning)
½ tsp thyme powder
⅓ cup minced fresh parsley
¼ cup grated provolone
sourdough bread

Preheat oven to 350°F.

Cut the sourdough bread into ½-inch slices and lightly toast it.

Heat the olive oil and butter in a medium frying pan. Sauté the garlic and onion until the onions are very limp. Stir in the seafood seasoning and thyme and sauté for another minute or so. Add the snails and parsley to the pan, cover and simmer over low heat for 20 minutes. Stir several times.

Place a snail into each slot of four escargot dishes and distribute the sauce equally over top. Sprinkle with the cheese and bake in the oven for 20 minutes or until the cheese has melted. Serve with sourdough bread.

Serves 4

Prawns and **okra**
on a BED OF SPINACH

1 lb	fresh prawns, shells, heads and tails removed
¾ lb	fresh okra, tops and tips removed, chopped
3 tbsp	butter
	salt
	ground black pepper
½	lime
1 cup	shredded fresh spinach

Heat the butter in a medium frying pan. Sauté the prawns and okra for 4 minutes. Add the salt and pepper and sauté for 5 minutes more.

Ladle the prawns and okra over the shredded spinach. Squeeze the lime juice over top and serve with baguette bread.

Serves 4

It's tough to find a faster hot appetizer than this one.

Okra used to be hard to find, but now that it's grown in several U.S. states and outside North America, it is available fresh most of the year.

MUSSELS in a cream sauce

I usually prefer my seafood in a light tomato sauce, but here is a cream sauce for mussels that I enjoy. When I'm planning a dinner, I try to follow a seafood appetizer such as this with a pork or chicken main dish.

36	mussels, cleaned and scrubbed
¾ cup	water
½ cup	dry white wine
¼ cup	minced shallots
2	large garlic cloves, minced
1 tsp	curry powder
½ tsp	coriander powder
¼ tsp	cumin powder
⅛ tsp	cayenne pepper
1½ cups	whipping cream
2 tbsp	fresh tarragon, shredded
	paprika
2	Portuguese buns, quartered and oven-toasted

Bring the water, wine, shallots and garlic to a boil in a pot large enough to hold the mussels. Remove from the heat and stir in the curry, coriander, cumin and cayenne. Add the mussels, return the pan to the heat, cover and simmer for 5 to 8 minutes or until the mussels open. Discard any that do not open.

Divide the mussels among four shallow soup bowls. Stir the cream and tarragon into the stock and bring to a low simmer. Ladle the sauce over the mussels and sprinkle with paprika. Serve with the toasted Portuguese buns.

Serves 4

rock lobster FRITTERS
with fresh tomato salsa

¾ lb	rock lobster, coarsely chopped
2 cups	flour
2	large eggs, well beaten
¼ cup	milk
¼ cup	beer
2 tbsp	baking soda
1 tsp	thyme powder
1 tsp	coriander powder
½ tsp	ground black pepper
½ tsp	salt
4 cups	olive oil, approximately
¼ cup	minced fresh cilantro
	Fresh Tomato Salsa (see p 154)
	lime wedges

A treat for lobster lovers. This appetizer makes for a great lead-in for a main course.

You can replace the rock lobster with uncooked fresh shrimp meat. Make the Fresh Tomato Salsa beforehand.

Combine the flour, eggs, milk, beer and baking soda in a large bowl. Stir in the thyme, coriander, pepper and salt. Fold the chopped rock lobster into this batter.

Put olive oil to a depth of 1 ½ inches in a frying pan and heat it to 250 to 275° F.

Scoop the batter, 1 ½ tablespoons for each scoop, into the hot oil. Do not overfill the pan as the temperature will drop too fast. Keep turning the fritters until they are golden brown. Drain them and place in a single layer on a serving platter and sprinkle with the cilantro. Serve with the Fresh Tomato Salsa and lime wedges.

Serves 4

SALMON BALLS
with shrimp and hot sauce

My mother used to serve a simpler version of this appetizer for dinner with boiled potatoes and a fresh green salad. I've added shrimp and hot sauce to her recipe.

I prefer canned salmon because left-over salmon may impart a fishy taste to this dish.

2 cans	(7 ½ oz each) sockeye salmon, drained; skin and bones discarded
¼ lb	shrimp meat, minced
2 tbsp	minced fresh parsley
¼ tsp	Tabasco sauce
2	large eggs
	flour
4 cups	olive oil, approximately

Combine the salmon, shrimp meat, parsley and hot sauce in a bowl. Add the eggs, blending them well into the mixture. Stir in the flour a little at a time until the mixture starts to thicken. The texture should be that of a dumpling mix, thick but not runny or lumpy.

Put ½ inch of olive oil in a frying pan and bring to 250 to 275°F. Using a soup spoon, take scoops of the salmon mixture (about 1 ½-inches in diameter) and fry in the hot oil until they turn a golden brown on all sides.

Place on paper towels for a few moments to drain and then serve.

Serves 4 to 6

Chicken-or-the-egg appetizer

4	boneless chicken breast halves, skinned
	ground black pepper
8	thin slices Black Forest ham
4	small eggs, hard-boiled and shelled
	flour
3 tbsp	olive oil
1/4 cup	water

The presentation of this dish has always gotten raves. The beauty of the dish from the chef's point of view is that it can be prepared well in advance and served at room temperature.

Flatten the chicken breasts by pounding between wax paper to twice their size. Sprinkle with pepper. Put two pieces of ham on each flattened chicken breast, covering the entire breast. Place an egg on the narrow end and roll it so the egg is wrapped in the chicken breast. Stick two toothpicks through the middle of each breast to hold it together.

Heat the olive oil in a medium frying pan. Dredge the rolled chicken breast in flour and fry until all sides are browned well and the chicken is completely cooked. Remove from the frying pan, wrap in plastic food wrap and set aside.

Add the water to the frying pan and scrape up all the browned chicken particles off the bottom of the pan. Simmer for 2 to 5 minutes, strain and transfer the sauce to a small saucepan.

When the chicken reaches room temperature, remove the toothpicks, slice into 3/8-inch rounds and arrange on a serving platter. Heat the sauce and dot each chicken round with 1/4 teaspoon of sauce.

Serves 4

Mama's PARTY crab dip

When our parents were having relatives over, Mama made so much of this dip that my sister, brother, cousins and I got to indulge ourselves.

⅓ cup	butter
¾ cup	flour
1	quart half-and-half cream
3 lbs	crab meat, bits of shell removed
8	large eggs, hard-boiled and chopped
½ cup	minced parsley
½ cup	chopped green onions
2 tbsp	chopped roasted red bell peppers (see page 152)
2	large garlic cloves, minced
1 tsp	salt
¼ tsp	cayenne pepper

Melt and heat the butter in a large pot. Stir in the flour and sauté until well blended, making sure it does not change in colour. (This is a white roux).

Gradually add the cream, stirring continuously and cooking until the mixture thickens. Add the crab, eggs, parsley, green onions, red peppers, garlic, salt and cayenne pepper, stirring very gently to blend them well.

Remove to a serving bowl and serve as a hot dip or refrigerate to serve later. If served as a cold dip, bring to room temperature to heighten the flavour.

Serves 8 to 12

Pasta APPETIZER
with parsley and olives

⅓ cup	olive oil, divided
3	medium shallots, minced
2	large garlic cloves, minced
⅛ tsp	dried and crushed red chilies
1 cup	chopped fresh parsley
½ cup	minced green olives
½ tbsp	raspberry vinegar
2 tbsp	lightly toasted pine nuts
¾ lb	pasta, wide noodles

Garlic, green olives, raspberry vinegar and pine nuts. This odd combination makes a definite statement among pasta sauces.

Prepare a sauce by heating 2 tablespoons of olive oil in a medium frying pan. Sauté the shallots and garlic until the shallots become limp, making sure the garlic does not burn. Add the remaining olive oil, red chilies, parsley, green olives and raspberry vinegar to the frying pan and simmer for 5 minutes.

Cook the pasta, drain well and put on individual appetizer plates. Spoon equal amounts of the heated sauce over top and sprinkle with toasted pine nuts.

Serves 4

spinach ball appetizers

A great appetizer for an informal party, served either hot or at room temperature. Of the oven stuffing mixes on the market, I prefer the Brownberry brand.

3 pkgs	(10 oz each) fresh spinach
4 cups	oven stuffing mix
1 cup	butter, melted
1 cup	minced white onion
1/2 cup	freshly grated Parmesan
4 tbsp	sweet hot sauce (e.g., Tiger Sauce)
3	large garlic cloves, minced
1 tsp	coriander powder
1 tsp	salt
1/2 tsp	thyme powder
6	large eggs
2 cups	fine bread crumbs

Preheat oven to 325 to 350°F.

Chop all the spinach. Simmer it with a minimum amount of water in a large pot until tender. Drain it well.

Combine the spinach, stuffing mix, butter and onion in a bowl. Add the Parmesan, sweet hot sauce, garlic, coriander, salt and thyme and blend well. Add the eggs and bread crumbs, mixing and blending all the ingredients well. If the mixture is too sloppy, add more bread crumbs a little at a time.

Shape the mixture into balls, 1 inch to 1 1/4 inches in diameter. Arrange on a greased cookie sheet and bake in the oven for 25 to 35 minutes. Transfer to a large serving platter and serve at room temperature.

Yields 20 to 28

Papa's PERFECT steamed clams

40 butter clams, scrubbed and washed
½ cup minced fresh parsley
8 large garlic cloves, minced
fine bread crumbs
ground black pepper
salt
¼ cup olive oil
1½ cups water
parsley sprigs

Put a layer of clams in the bottom of a large pot. Sprinkle with parsley, garlic, bread crumbs, pepper and a little salt. Repeat this until you run out of clams, finishing off with the bread crumbs and spices.

Drizzle the oil over the clams and then add the water by pouring it down the sides of the pot, not over the ingredients. Steam the clams over high heat for 15 to 20 minutes until they open.

Place the clams in individual deep soup bowls, stir the broth and ladle over the clams, topping with sprigs of parsley.

Serves 4

This is a first-class appetizer for a seafood dinner, although my family and I enjoy these clams as a main course. They can be prepared in the kitchen, on the side burner of your barbecue, in the backyard on a camp stove, or even over an open fire at the beach. My dad served them with Portuguese buns to soak up all the broth.

Please don't try to improve the broth by adding wine. Why tamper with perfection?

Shrimp
with jalapeño and garlic

In a hurry? This treatment is simple, delicious and leaves you more time to prepare your main dish. Try to buy large shrimp which will be sweet enough to offset the heat of the jalapeño.

2 doz   large fresh shrimp, heads removed, shells left on
2 tbsp   olive oil
6   large garlic cloves, minced
1/4 cup   clam nectar or juice
1   medium jalapeño pepper, minced
1/4 cup   butter
  ground black pepper

Heat the olive oil in a large frying pan. Add the shrimp and sauté until they turn pink. Stir in the garlic, clam nectar or juice and the jalapeño and simmer for 3 minutes. Add the butter and cook only long enough to melt the butter. Arrange the prawns and the sauce in a shallow serving dish. Sprinkle liberally with pepper and serve with Portuguese buns.

Serves 4

SOUPS & CHOWDERS

Clam chowder
with bacon, okra and tomatoes

A red clam chowder for a chilly November evening. Most people think of clam chowder as a cream-based soup. I say be adventurous and go red. The okra gives a slightly different taste and is a natural thickener.

5	medium unpeeled Yukon gold potatoes
1 ½ lbs	fresh clam meat
3 cups	clam nectar or juice
½ lb	double-smoked bacon, finely chopped
2	celery hearts (the tender, inner ribs and leaves), chopped
1	medium white onion, minced
1 cup	chopped fresh okra
1 tbsp	ground black pepper (or to taste)
1 tsp	salt
1 tsp	dried and crushed red chilies
¼ tsp	thyme powder
1 can	(28 oz) plum tomatoes, drained and chopped
4–6 cups	V8 Vegetable Cocktail

Cover the unpeeled potatoes with water in a large pot and bring to a boil. Lower the heat to a simmer and cook until done. Drain the potatoes and place in cold water to stop the cooking process. Remove the skins, cut the potatoes into 1-inch cubes, put into a bowl and set aside.

Chop the clam meat and put into a small saucepan. Add the clam nectar or juice, cover and simmer for 5 to 10 minutes until the meat is tender. Remove from the heat and set aside.

Sauté the bacon in a large pot until crisp. Add the celery and onion and sauté for 10 minutes. Stir in the okra and sauté for 5 minutes more. Stir in the pepper, salt, red chilies, thyme and tomatoes. Blend well and simmer for 5 minutes.

Add the clam meat with the clam nectar and just enough V8 juice to achieve a chowder consistency. Cover and simmer for half an hour.

Stir in the diced potatoes, replace the lid and simmer just long enough to heat the potatoes thoroughly. Serve with a heavy sourdough bread.

Serves 6 to 8

Shellfish BISQUE
with clams, mussels and crab

12 large clams, washed and scrubbed
12 large mussels, washed and scrubbed
½ lb crab meat
3 tbsp butter
1 large carrot, minced
1 medium onion, chopped
¾ cup white rice
¼ tsp sage powder
¼ tsp savory powder
¼ tsp thyme powder
water
1 cup clam nectar or juice
¼ cup brandy
½ tbsp ground black pepper
½ tsp salt
⅔ cup whipping cream
2 tbsp minced fresh parsley

All the ingredients in this recipe can be easily found at any time of the year. The bisque can be made in the morning and served for dinner at room temperature or reheated. Be sure to keep it chilled on a summer day.

Heat the butter in a large pot. Add the carrot and onion, and sauté until the onion is golden brown. Add the clams, mussels, rice and herbs and cover with cold water. Bring the water to a boil, lower the heat to medium, cover the pot and simmer until the rice is soft, about 35 minutes.

Take the clams and mussels from the pot. Remove the meat and discard the shells. In a food processor, purée the meat, the contents of the pot, the crab meat and clam nectar or juice. Return the purée to the cooking pot. Stir in the brandy, pepper and salt. Bring to a simmer. When heated, remove from the heat and allow to stand for 5 minutes.

Stir in the cream. Reheat the bisque but do not bring to a boil. Transfer to a soup tureen and garnish with parsley.

Serves 6 to 8

Yukon gold
POTATO AND LEEK SOUP

First the French made a creamy leek and potato soup. Then an American chef added chicken broth, served it cold and called it vichyssoise. Now here's a Canadian contribution – those wonderful Yukon gold potatoes in a hot combination with leeks.

5 large leeks, washed, trimmed and minced
4 large Yukon gold potatoes, peeled and thinly sliced
1 medium white onion, diced
5 tbsp butter
1 tbsp flour
4 cups chicken broth
1 cup whipping cream
paprika

Heat the butter in a large pot. Add the leeks, potatoes and onions. Sauté for 30 to 40 minutes until the vegetables are tender. Add the flour and sauté over medium heat for 5 minutes more. Remove from the heat and stir in 1 cup of the chicken broth.

Purée the mixture in a food processor or blender. Return the purée to the pot, stir in the remaining chicken broth and bring to a gentle boil. Reduce the heat and simmer for 30 minutes, stirring occasionally.

Stir in the cream and cook the soup until it is just heated. Ladle into a tureen and sprinkle with paprika.

Serves 4

SHRIMP SOUP
with rice and mushrooms

2 tbsp   olive oil
2 tbsp   grated fresh ginger
½ tsp   dried and crushed red chilies
5 cups   chicken broth
½ cup   basmati rice
1 lb   hand-peeled large shrimp meat
8   large shiitake mushrooms, quartered
½ cup   unsweetened coconut milk
3 tbsp   fresh lime juice
½ cup   coarsely chopped green onions

A spicy Asian soup that can be ready to serve in 40 minutes. A good starter before a curried dish.

Heat the olive oil in a large pot, add the ginger and red chilies and sauté for about 2 minutes. Add the chicken broth and bring to a boil. Stir in the rice, cover, lower the heat and simmer until the rice is tender.

Stir in the shrimp, mushrooms and coconut milk. Simmer until the shrimp are done, about 5 to 7 minutes.

Remove from the heat and stir in the lime juice. Garnish with the green onions.

Serves 4

SHRIMP étoufée cajun-style

Not all food from Louisiana is burning hot. The Cajuns, who are descended from French-speaking immigrants from Acadia, have a different cuisine. Typical of their dishes is this milder étoufée, which is basically a gumbo.

The large shrimp that the Cajuns use are not available fresh in many areas. They can be replaced with medium-sized prawns, which may not be as sweet.

Serve with brown rice.

2 lbs	fresh, large shrimp, heads and shells removed
1/4 lb	butter
1/3 cup	olive oil
1/2 cup	flour
2	large leeks, white ends only, diced
1	large green pepper, diced
2 cups	chopped celery leaves
4	large garlic cloves, minced
1 tbsp	ground black pepper
1 tbsp	coriander powder
1/2 tsp	white pepper
1 can	(28 oz) plum tomatoes, puréed
5 cups	clam nectar or juice
1 tsp	habanero hot sauce
4	shallots, minced

Heat the butter and olive oil in a large pot. Stir in the flour and sauté over medium heat, creating a dark brown roux. Add the leeks, green pepper, celery and garlic. Sauté for 5 minutes. Stir in the pepper, coriander and white pepper. Sauté for 2 minutes more. Add the tomato purée and stir until well blended.

Slowly add the clam nectar or juice, stirring well to blend in with the roux. Add the habanero hot sauce, cover and simmer for 30 minutes.

Fold the shrimp into the étoufée, replace the lid and simmer until the shrimp are done in 3 to 4 minutes. Serve over brown rice sprinkled with the shallots.

Serves 4

Avocado BISQUE

3	large ripe avocados, seeded, peeled and chopped
1 bunch	fresh spinach, washed and trimmed
1 cup	chicken broth
10 oz	canned evaporated milk
1 tbsp	sweet hot sauce (e.g., Tiger Sauce)
1/2 tsp	onion salt
1/4 tsp	ground black pepper
	paprika
1/2 lb	bacon slices, crisp-fried, drained and crumbled

In this recipe, nothing works as well as canned milk, which is sweeter than whole milk and not as rich as cream. Serve the bisque hot, at room temperature or chilled.

Steam the spinach for 2 to 3 minutes. Transfer to a food processor or blender, along with the avocados and chicken broth and purée. Blend in the evaporated milk.

Put into a medium saucepan and keep warm over a low heat. Stir in the sweet hot sauce, onion salt and pepper and simmer about 3 to 5 minutes, just long enough to heat all the ingredients.

Ladle into individual soup bowls and sprinkle liberally with paprika. Sprinkle the bacon over top.

Serves 4

Corn chowder with **bacon** and **potatoes**

Rather than water, I use chicken broth or vegetable broth in many of my soups and gumbos. It adds flavour. You should not have to add salt.

2 cans	(10 oz each) cream-style corn
1/2 lb	bacon slices, chopped
2	medium leeks, white ends only, minced
1/2 cup	diced celery hearts and (the tender, inside ribs and leaves)
2 tbsp	butter
1 tbsp	flour
2 1/2 cups	chicken broth, kept warm over low heat
4	small white potatoes
1 tsp	ground black pepper
2	large eggs, lightly beaten
	salt to taste

Fry the bacon in a large pot. When it begins to crisp, add the onions and celery and sauté until tender. Stir in the flour and sauté over medium heat, creating a blond roux. Add the warm chicken broth, stirring and blending well. Remove from the heat and set aside.

Boil the potatoes until tender. Drain, peel and dice the potatoes, adding them to the chicken broth.

Bring the chowder to a simmer. Stir in the corn and pepper and simmer for 10 minutes. Drizzle the beaten egg into the chowder, stirring constantly so that the drizzled egg cooks like a thin noodle. Simmer for 2 minutes before serving.

Serves 4 to 6

Red bell pepper
soup with buttermilk

4	large red bell peppers
2 cups	chicken broth
4	large leeks, white ends only, minced
1 tsp	dried and crushed red chilies
2 cups	fat-free buttermilk
	ground black pepper
4 slices	baguette bread, ¾-inch thick
2 tbsp	olive oil
	salt
1 tbsp	minced fresh parsley

Preheat oven to 350 to 400°F.

Halve the peppers lengthwise and remove the stems and seeds. Roast the pepper halves over a gas flame, under a broiler or on your barbecue until the skin is charred and bubbling. Place in a plastic bag and allow to cool. Peel the skin away from the peppers and discard. Place the meat and any juices into a bowl and set aside.

Bring the chicken broth and leeks to a boil in a saucepan, lower the heat and simmer 20 minutes. Stir in the roasted red peppers and simmer for half an hour.

Transfer the mixture to a blender or food processor and purée until smooth. Return the soup to the pot, add the red chilies and bring to a low simmer.

Brush the baguette slices with the olive oil. Sprinkle each one with salt and some parsley. Place on a cookie sheet and toast for 12 to 18 minutes in the oven until lightly browned and crisp. Remove and set aside.

Stir the buttermilk into the soup. When it begins to simmer, remove from the heat and ladle into 4 soup bowls. Sprinkle with pepper and the remaining parsley. Float a slice of the toasted baguette bread on each bowl.

Serves 4

Soups similar to this are served throughout Portugal, Spain, and along the Adriatic coast. Rather than using purchased roasted red bell peppers, I always roast my own for this recipe because I find I get a richer bell-pepper taste.

Creamed asparagus soup

Smooth and creamy – an asparagus lover's delight. The Yukon gold potatoes and the fresh tarragon are the key ingredients in this soup.

2 lbs	fresh asparagus, trimmed, sliced into ½-inch pieces
6 tbsp	butter
3 tbsp	flour
2 ½ cups	peeled Yukon gold potatoes, in ½-inch cubes
1 cup	diced white onion
2	large garlic cloves, minced
1 tbsp	ground black pepper (or to taste)
½ tsp	coriander powder
4 cups	chicken broth
1 cup	light cream
1 tbsp	minced fresh parsley
1 tbsp	minced fresh tarragon

Heat the butter in a large pot. Stir in the flour and sauté over medium heat, creating a light blond roux. Add the potatoes, onion and garlic and sauté until the onion is very limp. Stir in the pepper and coriander, add the chicken broth and simmer for 30 to 40 minutes.

Transfer the soup to a food processor or blender and purée. Return the purée to the pot and bring to a low simmer. Add the asparagus and cook for 10 to 15 minutes until tender.

Stir in the cream, making sure you do not allow the soup to boil. Transfer to a soup tureen and sprinkle with the minced herbs.

Serves 8

FISH & SHELLFISH

Fisherman's prize
bouillabaisse

I developed this recipe for special occasions in my firehall. Now, when I'm asked to be a guest cook for a retirement dinner in any other firehall, this is the dish most often requested.

Essentially a bouillabaisse, this soup is made from ingredients abundant on the Pacific coast.

1 lb	red snapper fillets, in 4 equal pieces
12	fresh prawns, heads and shells removed, tails left on
12	mussels, scrubbed and washed
12	butter clams, scrubbed and washed
2	large leeks, finely chopped
6	large garlic cloves, minced
1 cup	finely chopped celery hearts (the tender, inner ribs)
1	large carrot, grated
1 can	(14 oz) plum tomatoes, drained and chopped
1/4 cup	and 2 tbsp olive oil
1 cup	clam nectar or juice
1 tbsp	thyme powder
1 tbsp	ground black pepper
1/2 tsp	salt
1/4 tsp	dried and crushed red chilies
	flour

To make a stock, place the prawn heads and shells in a medium pot. Add 1 1/2 cups water, bring to a boil and simmer for half an hour. Strain the stock and discard the heads and shells. Stir the clam nectar or juice into the stock and set aside.

Heat the 1/4 cup olive oil in a large pot. Sauté the leeks, garlic, celery hearts and carrots until the vegetables are well cooked. This will take about 30 minutes. Stir in the thyme, pepper, salt and chilies. Add the tomatoes and the stock, cover and bring to a boil. Lower the heat and simmer for 15 minutes.

Heat the 2 tablespoons of olive oil in a medium frying pan. Dust the red snapper pieces in flour and sauté until lightly browned. Put a piece of snapper in each of four deep-dish soup bowls and set aside. Bring the soup to a rapid boil, add the prawns, mussels and clams and cook for 6 to 8 minutes.

Distribute equal amounts of prawns, mussels and clams over each piece of fish. Ladle the stock and vegetables into each bowl and serve with lots of sourdough bread to sop up the stock. Serves 4

Salmon FILLETS twice-baked

2	salmon fillets (2 lbs each), deboned
½ cup	olive oil, divided
1 tbsp	ground black pepper (or to taste)
3	large leeks, minced
1	small white onion, minced
1	small celery heart, minced
4	garlic cloves, minced fine
1 tbsp	dried whole Mexican oregano
½ tsp	salt
1 cup	tomato sauce
4 cups	V8 Vegetable Cocktail
¾ lb	orzo

When my mother prepared this dish, she served it with a green salad with an oil and vinegar dressing and fresh French bread. Salmon fillets have small pin bones that should be removed with bone tweezers.

Preheat oven to 375°F.

Place ¼ cup of the olive oil in a baking dish. Arrange the salmon in the dish, sprinkle with the pepper and bake for 20 to 30 minutes.

Remove the salmon from the oven. Insert two spatulas between the skin and the flesh and lift the flesh off. Place the skinless fillets in a fresh baking dish.

Heat the remaining ¼ cup of olive oil in a medium saucepan. Sauté the leeks, onion and celery heart until limp. Stir in the garlic, oregano and salt and sauté for 5 minutes.

Add the tomato sauce and half the V8 juice, cover and simmer for half an hour, which should produce a thin red sauce. If it is too thick, add some V8 juice a little at a time.

Raise the oven to 400°F. Ladle the sauce over the fillets and bake for about 5 minutes or until the sauce begins to bubble around the edges. Then bake 5 minutes longer.

Meanwhile, cook the orzo in boiling water for about 10 minutes. Drain it and keep warm in a pot.

Lift the salmon fillets out of the sauce and place in the centre of a large serving platter. Pour the sauce into the orzo pot and heat slowly until hot, stirring often while bringing the heat up. Surround the fillets with the orzo.
Serves 8

Salmon sauté with
peppers, asparagus and ginger

This is one dish for which I prefer sockeye salmon. I use the back of the sockeye because it is much more solid and holds together better than the belly. Save the belly for the barbecue because the flavour and texture are remarkable and it won't dry out.

2 lbs	sockeye salmon, skinned, deboned, cut into 1 1/2-inch cubes
3 tbsp	olive oil
1	yellow bell pepper, seeds and membrane removed, cut into 1/4-inch strips
1 bunch	asparagus, cut into 1 1/2-inch lengths
2	whole green onions, sliced lengthwise into very thin strips
1/2 tsp	grated fresh ginger
1/4 tsp	ground black pepper
1	large lime, halved

Put all the marinade ingredients into a food processor and process on high speed until creamy.

Put the salmon cubes into a dish, pour the marinade over and refrigerate for 2 to 3 hours. Gently turn the salmon several times while it marinates.

Heat the olive oil in a medium frying pan. Using a slotted spoon, remove the salmon from the marinade and add to the hot oil. Sauté for 3 to 5 minutes, turning the pieces very gently. Remove with a slotted spoon and set aside.

Add the bell pepper and asparagus to the frying pan and sauté until tender. Stir in the green onions, ginger and pepper and sauté for 3 minutes more.

Return the salmon to the frying pan, toss very gently and cook until the salmon is heated through. Squeeze the lime juice over the top.

Serves 4

Marinade

1/4 cup	olive oil
2	large garlic cloves, chopped
1/2 tbsp	balsamic vinegar
1 tsp	sugar

Dungeness CRAB baked with celery hearts

4	live Dungeness crabs
2 tbsp	salt
½ cup	minced celery hearts (the tender inner ribs)
¼ cup	minced fresh parsley
1 tbsp	ground black pepper (or to taste)
¾ cup	fine bread crumbs, divided
¼ cup	olive oil, plus some extra

Preheat oven to 350°F.

Boil the crabs two at a time in a large pot in salted water for 18 minutes. Remove from the heat and allow the crabs to sit in the water for 5 minutes. Immerse the crabs in cold water to stop the cooking process.

Grasp the shells and lift them off. Wash the shells in hot water and set aside. Remove and discard all the shell tabs, tomalley and the gills. Rinse the body and legs under cold water. Remove all the meat from the legs and body cavity, trying to keep the meat in unbroken pieces. Set aside in a bowl.

Combine the chopped celery, parsley, pepper, ½ cup bread crumbs and ¼ cup olive oil with the crab meat. Toss gently. Fill the body shells with the crab mixture. Sprinkle with the remaining bread crumbs and drizzle with about ½ teaspoon olive oil.

Arrange the shells in a shallow baking dish and bake for 20 to 30 minutes or until the bread crumbs begin to brown.

Serves 4

If you prefer not to boil and clean crabs, you can purchase crab meat, but it won't be as sweet as meat from a freshly cooked crab.

Many fish markets can supply crab shells. If you cannot find any, use single-serving baking dishes.

Prawns marinated in **balsamic vinegar** and honey

The long marinating period will really sweeten up these morsels. The blend of balsamic vinegar, honey and shiitake mushrooms gives this prawn dish a very different flavour.

20 large fresh prawns, peeled and deveined
3 tbsp olive oil, divided
4 large shiitake mushrooms, coarsely chopped
3 large plum tomatoes, cut into eighths
1/2 small white onion, coarsely chopped
1/2 tbsp ground black pepper
1/4 tsp salt
1/4 tsp minced fresh cilantro
2 large limes, cut into 8 wedges

Combine the marinade ingredients in a shallow dish. Add the prawns, cover with plastic food wrap and refrigerate for 12 to 24 hours. Turn the prawns several times.

Before beginning to cook, heat oven to 400°F.

Put 1 1/2 tablespoons olive oil in a shallow roasting pan. Lift the prawns from the marinade to the pan and roast in the oven for 6 to 8 minutes.

Bring the marinade to a boil in a small saucepan, lower the heat and simmer.

Heat the remaining 1 1/2 tablespoons olive oil in a medium frying pan. Sauté the mushrooms, tomatoes, onion, pepper, salt and cilantro for 5 minutes.

Arrange 5 prawns in each of 4 shallow soup dishes. Distribute equal amounts of the sautéed vegetable over the prawns and spoon on the hot marinade. Garnish with the lime wedges. Serves 4

Marinade

1/2 cup olive oil
3 tbsp balsamic vinegar
2 tbsp liquid honey
1/2 tbsp ground black pepper
1/2 tsp salt
1/4 tsp dried whole Mexican oregano
1/4 tsp thyme powder

Pork medallions with red bell peppers and asparagus (p 106)

Georgia Peach lamb chops (p 103)

Prawns **Creole** in beer and butter

2 lbs fresh prawns, heads and shells left on
½ lb butter, divided
2 tbsp Creole Seasoning
2 large garlic cloves, minced
½ cup beer
2 tbsp fresh lime juice
1 tbsp Worcestershire sauce

Spicy styles of cooking were just coming into vogue on the West Coast when I created this Creole-inspired dish for a TV cooking show in Kelowna, British Columbia.

Melt ¼ pound of the butter in a medium frying pan. Sauté the prawns until they just begin to change colour. Stir in the Creole Seasoning and garlic and sauté for a minute. Add the beer, lime juice and Worcestershire sauce. Simmer for 3 minutes. Stir in the remaining butter and shake the pan until all the butter is melted and the sauce is creamy.

Serve with baguette bread to dip in the sauce.

Serves 4

Creole Seasoning

⅓ cup salt
¼ cup paprika
¼ cup granulated onion
4 tbsp black pepper
2 tbsp cayenne pepper
2 tbsp thyme powder
2 tbsp granulated garlic
1 tbsp dried whole Mexican oregano

Combine all the ingredients. Store in the refrigerator indefinitely.

Prawn pie New Orleans

Pastry baking is not my forte, but for a baker this dish will be as easy – as pie. In Louisiana, where I found the inspiration for this recipe, many different meats and fish are baked in shells or a phyllo-type pastry.

1 lb	fresh prawns, shelled and cleaned
1/4 cup	minced fresh parsley
2 tbsp	port wine
1 pie shell (9 inches)	
1/4 lb	shiitaki mushrooms, sliced
3	large eggs
1 cup	whipping cream
1/2 tsp	ground black pepper
1/2 tsp	coriander powder
1/4 tsp	salt
1/4 tsp	white pepper
1/4 cup	fine bread crumbs

Combine the prawns, parsley and port wine in a bowl and refrigerate overnight.

The next day, following directions for your own pastry or for a frozen pie shell, partially bake the shell until the bottom has just started to get flaky.

Before beginning to prepare the filling, heat oven to 450°F.

Discard the port and parsley and lightly steam the prawns for about 6 minutes. Transfer to a bowl.

Sauté the mushrooms in a medium nonstick frying pan until they are limp and all liquid has evaporated. Set aside and allow to cool.

Beat the eggs in a bowl. Whisk in the cream, black pepper, coriander, salt and white pepper. Stir in the prawns and cooled mushrooms. Pour into the partially cooked pastry shell. Sprinkle the bread crumbs over the top.

Bake for 10 minutes. Reduce the heat to 400°F and bake for 10 minutes. Reduce the heat to 350°F and bake for a final 10 minutes.

Serves 4

Rock SHRIMP SAUTÉ
with asparagus, corn and papaya

1 ½ lbs	rock shrimp
½ cup	fresh asparagus tips, in 1-inch pieces
1 cup	canned peaches-and-cream corn niblets, drained
½ cup	papaya, in ½-inch cubes
½ cup	honeydew melon, in ½-inch cubes
2 tbsp	olive oil
1 tbsp	hot sauce (e.g., Melinda's XXXtra Hot Sauce)
1 tbsp	sweet hot sauce (e.g., Tiger Sauce)
1 tsp	ground black pepper
½ tsp	dried whole Mexican oregano
½ tsp	coriander powder
¼ tsp	salt
1	lime

Rock shrimp, which I used to buy in five-pound frozen packages, are now available thawed in smaller quantities at fish markets. Their price is comparable to that of large shrimp.

Heat the olive oil in a large frying pan. Sauté the rock shrimp and asparagus tips for 2 minutes. Stir in the two hot sauces, pepper, oregano, coriander and salt. Sauté for 3 minutes or until the rock lobster turns pink.

Add the corn niblets, papaya and honeydew melon to the pan. Stir gently and cover with a tight-fitting lid. Remove from the heat and allow to stand for 2 to 3 minutes, just to heat the fruit.

Remove the lid, place the pan on a high heat and cook until the mixture begins to sizzle. Spoon onto a large serving platter and squeeze the lime juice over top.

Serves 4

Oysters in a **spicy butter** and **cream** sauce

Because it departs from the usual deep-frying or breading of oysters, I have found that this dish is welcomed by oyster lovers. Also it is quick and easy to prepare.

24	small shucked oysters, liquid reserved
8	slices bacon
½ lb	butter, divided
⅓ cup	minced shallots
½ tbsp	ground black pepper
⅛ tsp	dried and crushed red chilies
¾ cup	dry white wine
¼ cup	whipping cream
¼ cup	minced green onions, white ends only

Preheat oven to 200 °F.

Fry the bacon slices until crisp. Crumble them.

Heat ½ tablespoon of the bacon fat and ¼ pound of the butter in a large frying pan. Sauté the oysters over high heat for about 2 minutes. Transfer them to a baking dish large enough to hold them in one layer only and keep warm in the oven.

Sauté the shallots in the frying pan until limp. Stir in the pepper, red chilies and wine and sauté for 2 to 3 minutes.

Add the remaining butter and oyster liquid to the pan and bring to a low simmer. Stir in the whipping cream, holding a low simmer and making sure the sauce does not boil.

Gently fold the oysters into the sauce and just cook until the oysters are heated.

Put 6 oysters into each of 4 deep-dished soup bowls. Ladle the sauce over top and serve with sourdough bread.

Serves 4

OYSTERS hickory-seasoned and deep-fried

48	small shucked oysters, drained
½ cup	flour
¼ cup	chili powder
1 tbsp	garlic powder
1 tsp	cayenne pepper
½ tsp	salt
½ tsp	hickory-smoked salt
9 cups	oil for deep-frying

Put the flour, chili powder, garlic powder, cayenne and the two salts into a medium-sized brown paper bag and shake to blend.

Add the oysters to the bag one or two at a time. Shake to coat the oysters with the spices.

For deep-frying you will want oil to a depth of 2 ½ inches in a pot at least twice that depth. Heat the oil to 350 to 370° F and deep-fry the oysters in batches for 3 to 5 minutes.

Serves 4

Buy the oysters already shucked, but ask your fishmonger for twenty-four oyster shells. To serve, put two oysters into each shell. Hickory-smoked salt really enhances the flavour of oysters. If you use a Chinese wire spoon to lift the oysters, very little oil will cling to them.

CLAMS in a spicy
tomato broth with garlic baguette

This goes beyond simply steaming clams. One baguette may seem like a lot for four people, but with this dish you'll want it to soak up the broth. You'll want to prepare the baked garlic cloves first. Add a green salad and you have a meal.

80	butter clams, washed and scrubbed
1 lb	spicy pork sausage meat
3 tbsp	olive oil
3	large garlic cloves, coarsely minced
½ cup	minced fresh parsley, divided
1 tsp	dried and crushed red chilies
½ can	beer
1 can	(14 oz) plum tomatoes, drained and puréed

Heat the olive oil in a large pot and fry the sausage meat until it is browned. Stir in the clams, garlic, ¼ cup of the parsley and red chilies. Cover the pot and cook for 2 minutes. Add the beer and simmer without a lid until the liquid is reduced to half.

Stir in the tomato purée, replace the lid and steam until all the clams have opened. This will take about 6 to 8 minutes.

Transfer the clams, sausage meat and broth to a large serving bowl, sprinkle with the remaining parsley and serve with Garlic Baguette.

Serves 4

Garlic Baguette

1 loaf	baguette bread, in 1-inch slices
¼ cup	olive oil, approximately
4	large garlic heads
	ground black pepper

Preheat oven to 300°F. Place the garlic heads on separate pieces of aluminum foil. Drizzle with a little oil and wrap tightly. Bake for about 45 minutes. When cool enough to handle, squeeze the baked garlic cloves into a small bowl and mash with a fork.

Brush the slices of bread with olive oil. Toast in the oven until both sides are golden brown. Spread roasted garlic on each slice and sprinkle with pepper.

Lobster

Louisiana with lime juice

2	live lobsters (2 lbs each)
1 tbsp	olive oil
1/4 cup	minced shallots
1 tbsp	minced fresh parsley
1/3 cup	butter
1/2 cup	fine bread crumbs
1 tbsp	sweet hot sauce (e.g., Tiger Sauce)
1 tbsp	fresh lime juice
1/2 tbsp	ground black pepper
1/2 tsp	salt
3 tbsp	melted butter

This dish resembles one that is served all along the coast of the Gulf of Mexico from Corpus Christi to New Orleans. I have added shallots, hot sauce and lime juice.

Preheat oven to 325°F.

Put enough water to cover the lobsters into a very large pot, add about a tablespoon of salt and bring the water to a boil. Plunge the lobsters headfirst into the boiling water and cook for 8 minutes, counting from the time they enter the water. Remove the lobsters and cool them in a large quantity of cold water. (I fill my kitchen sink.)

Heat the olive oil in a medium pan and sauté the shallots until they are limp. Stir in the parsley, add the 1/3 cup butter and cook until the butter melts.

Remove the pan from the heat, stir in the bread crumbs, sweet hot sauce, lime juice, pepper and salt and set aside.

Break off the claws and remove the meat from them in one piece. With a serrated knife, cut the lobsters in half lengthwise. Remove the tomalley from the heads and blend it and most of the melted butter into the bread crumb mixture.

Arrange the lobster halves in a baking dish. Spread some bread crumb mixture over each one and top decoratively with one intact piece of claw meat. Brush the claw meat with the remaining melted butter. Place the dish on the lowest rack of the oven and bake for 15 minutes. Turn on the oven broiler and broil until the bread crumbs begin to brown.

Serves 4

Skate salad dinner

Skate is among the most underrated of seafoods, but if you enjoy scallops, you will enjoy skate. You could serve this salad with boiled potatoes or cooked cornmeal, which won't compete with the delicate flavour of the fish.

Another way of preparing skate is to dust it lightly in flour and panfry in olive oil.

2 lbs	fresh skate, skin removed
1/3 cup	olive oil
1/2 cup	minced celery
1/4 cup	minced green onion
3	large garlic cloves, minced
2 tbsp	minced fresh parsley
1 tbsp	ground black pepper (or to taste)
1/4 cup	finely chopped arugula
1/4 tbsp	salt
2 tbsp	fresh lime juice

Cut the skate wings into workable pieces and arrange in a large frying pan. Add 1 cup of water, cover and poach for about 10 minutes until the fish is tender. Remove with a slotted spoon and set aside to cool.

Remove the meat by sliding a dinner knife down each side of the cartilage. Cut the meat into bite-size pieces and place in a large serving bowl.

Prepare the dressing by combining the olive oil, celery, green onion, garlic, parsley, pepper, salt and arugula in a bowl. Allow to sit at room temperature for 15 minutes.

Ladle the dressing over the skate, add the lime juice and gently toss, making sure not to bruise or break the skate meat.

Serves 4

Red snapper
fillets with ginger and tomatoes

4 pieces	red snapper (2 halved 1-lb fillets)
1 ¼ cups	pecans, divided
½ cup	fine bread crumbs
	flour
3	large eggs, beaten
⅓ cup	olive oil, divided
1 tbsp	finely grated fresh ginger
5	large plum tomatoes, skinned and diced
½ cup	coarsely chopped green onions
1 tsp	ground black pepper
¼ tsp	salt

A fancier way of preparing one of the most widely purchased white fish in the world. The ginger sauce brings this dish to perfection.

Preheat oven to 325°F.

Measure ¾ cup pecans. Toast them until crisp and then purée in a food processor or blender. Cut the remaining ½ cup pecans into quarters. Roast these pieces and keep them hot while the fish is cooking.

Combine the bread crumbs and puréed pecans in a dish. Coat the fillets with flour, dip into the beaten egg and then into the bread crumb and pecan mixture, pressing the mixture well into the fillets.

Arrange the fish pieces in a single layer on wax paper. Heat half the olive oil in a medium frying pan. Fry the fillets until both sides are golden brown. Transfer to a baking dish in one layer and keep warm in the oven.

Prepare the sauce by adding the remaining olive oil to the frying pan. Stir in 1 tablespoon flour and 1 tablespoon of the bread-crumb and pecan mixture and sauté over medium heat, creating a tan roux. At the same time, scrape any browned fish particles off the bottom of the pan.

Add the ginger and sauté for 2 to 3 minutes. Stir in the tomatoes, green onion, salt and pepper and cook only until the tomatoes are heated through. If the mixture is too thick, add a little hot water for a slow-running sauce.

Place a fillet on each of four dinner plates and ladle on some sauce. Sprinkle with the pecan pieces. Serves 4

Summertime TUNA SALAD

FOR TWO

*This one is great for a
lazy summer day.
The oyster sauce
gives it a slight Asian
flair. Pay the extra
for solid white tuna;
this salad is worth it.*

2 cans	(6.5 oz each) solid white tuna
2 cups	romaine lettuce, torn into bite-size pieces
1 cup	bean sprouts
1	small red bell pepper, diced
6	green onions, sliced thinly, lengthwise
3 tbsp	fresh lime juice
1 tbsp	olive oil
1 tbsp	oyster sauce
1 tbsp	fresh lime zest
1	small jalapeño pepper, minced

Combine the bean sprouts, bell pepper, green onions, lime juice, olive oil, oyster sauce, lime zest and jalapeño in a bowl.

Drain the tuna and break it into bite-size chunks or flakes. Gently fold the tuna into the dressing and allow to stand at room temperature for 15 minutes.

Arrange the romaine on two dinner plates. Gently toss the tuna mixture and spoon equal amounts over each bed of lettuce. Serve with a nice crusty bun and a light white wine.

Serves 2

BEEF, LAMB & PORK

Beef tenderloin with shiitake mushrooms

The double-smoked bacon and shiitake mushrooms set this one apart. A special-occasion dish with costly ingredients, this recipe demands some extra effort but is well worth it.

1	beef tenderloin (3 lbs)
2 tbsp	olive oil, divided
1/2 tsp	ground black pepper
1/4 tsp	salt
1/4 tsp	rosemary powder
1/3 cup	red wine
10	slices double-smoked bacon
1 1/2 lbs	shiitake mushrooms, coarsely chopped

Preheat oven to 450°F.

Place 1 tablespoon olive oil in a shallow baking dish. Put the tenderloin on top of the oil, tucking the thin end under. Sprinkle with the pepper, salt and rosemary. Cover the meat with the bacon strips and roast in the oven for about 30 minutes. Remove the bacon and reserve it. Pour the wine over the beef, reduce the oven temperature to 350°F and roast for 30 minutes more.

Chop the bacon. Heat the second tablespoon of olive oil in a medium frying pan and sauté the mushrooms for 10 minutes. Stir in the bacon and sauté for 5 minutes more.

Remove the tenderloin from the oven. Place it in the centre of a large serving platter and carve at 1/2-inch intervals. Surround the beef with the mushrooms, spoon any liquid from the baking dish over top and garnish with parsley.

Serves 4

Beef tenderloin marinated in rum

1	beef tenderloin (3 lbs)
¼ cup	amber rum
¼ cup	Demerara sugar
¼ cup	HP Sauce
3	large garlic cloves, minced
1 tbsp	finely grated fresh ginger
1 tbsp	ground black pepper
1 tbsp	coarse sea salt

Combine the rum, sugar, HP Sauce, garlic and ginger in a small saucepan. Cook over low heat, just until the sugar is dissolved. Remove the mixture from the heat and allow to reach room temperature. Place the tenderloin in a shallow dish, pour the marinade over top and refrigerate for 12 to 24 hours. Turn and baste with the marinade several times during this period.

Before beginning to cook, heat oven to 475°F.

Remove the tenderloin from the marinade and pat dry with a paper towel. Rub the entire roast with the pepper and the salt. Place the roast in an oiled, shallow roasting pan and roast in the oven for 15 minutes.

Turn the roast over and cook for 10 to 15 minutes more or until an instant-read thermometer reaches 150°F when inserted into the centre of the roast. This will produce a rare to medium roast, which is the optimum degree of doneness for this cut of beef. Slice at least 1 inch thick to serve.

Serves 4

Expecting a busy day tomorrow? You can do most of the work of this recipe a day ahead of time. In fact, it requires a 12- to 24-hour period to marinate.

If HP sauce is unavailable, substitute ⅛ cup of Worcestershire sauce.

Steak panfried with glazed vegetables

Celery root or cele-
riac is related to cel-
ery and tastes like it
but only the root is
eaten. It can be
grated raw for a
salad or cooked.
Scrub the root well
and pare off the
outer thick skin.

 2 New York strip steaks (8 oz each), trimmed of fat
 6 large garlic cloves, minced
 2 tbsp and ¼ cup olive oil
 8 small white potatoes, quartered
 12 small mushrooms, stems removed
 1 small celery root, cleaned and trimmed
 1 tbsp fresh lime juice

Preheat oven to 350°F.

Sprinkle both sides of the steak with salt and pepper, spread equal amounts of garlic on top of each steak and place in a shallow dish. Pour the 2 tablespoons oil over top, cover with plastic food wrap and allow to sit at room temperature for 45 minutes, turning the steaks several times.

Coarsely grate the celery root and place in a small bowl. Stir in the lime juice, cover with cold water and set aside.

Put ¼ cup of olive oil and the potato quarters into a baking dish and roast at 350°F for about 45 minutes. Turn the potatoes several times to allow all sides to get crisp.

When you are ready to cook the steaks, drain the olive oil from them into a medium frying pan and bring to a high heat. Sear the steaks well on both sides. Lower the heat to medium and fry them on each side for 3 minutes. Remove from the pan and keep warm.

Put the mushroom caps and 2 tablespoons of water into the frying pan. Cover and sauté for 5 minutes, shaking the pan to turn the caps and to release all the garlic and browned particles off the bottom of the pan. Remove the mushrooms with a slotted spoon and keep warm.

Drain the celery root well, put into the frying pan, cover and cook for 2 minutes.

Return the mushrooms to the pan and cook until heated. Drain the potatoes, discarding the oil.

Arrange a steak and some potatoes on individual dinner plates. Ladle celery root and mushrooms over each steak.

Serves 2

Beef fillet roasted with FIGS, grapefruit and NECTARINES

1	beef tenderloin (2 lbs), trimmed
1/2 tbsp	meat seasoning spice
1/2 tsp	ground black pepper
5	large garlic cloves, minced
3 tbsp	olive oil, divided
1/2 cup	minced dried figs
1/2 tbsp	flour
1/4 cup	dry red wine
1 tbsp	water
1	Texas pink grapefruit
2	large nectarines, pitted, peeled and cut into wedges

I hear so many raves about this garlic and fruit combination. The aroma and sweetness of the figs make this dish unique.

This isn't just a summertime dish; fresh nectarines from Mexico arrive in January in my area.

Preheat oven to 400°F.

Peel the grapefruit and remove the white membrane and seeds. Separate the grapefruit into its sections and place in a bowl.

Rub the tenderloin with the meat seasoning, pepper and garlic. Heat 2 tablespoons of olive oil in a medium frying pan, add the tenderloin and sear over medium to high heat until well browned on all sides. Transfer to a heavy roasting pan and drizzle with the remaining 1 tablespoon oil, cover and place in the oven for half an hour.

Meanwhile, prepare a sauce by putting the minced figs in the frying pan. Sauté for about 5 minutes, scraping all the brown particles off the bottom of the pan. Stir in the flour and sauté over medium heat, creating a brown roux. Add the red wine and cook for 3 minutes. Remove from the heat and set aside.

After the fillet has been in the oven for half an hour, remove it to a serving platter, cover with plastic food wrap and keep warm.

Place the roasting pan on the stove element on medium heat. Lay the fruit pieces in the pan, cover and cook for 1 minute. Turn the fruit, replace the lid and cook for another minute. Remove the pan from the heat and allow the fruit

to steam covered for 3 minutes. Slice the roast crosswise in
$1/2$-inch slices and surround it with the grapefruit and nectarine pieces.

Stir the liquid from the roasting pan into the fig-and-
red-wine sauce and bring to a low simmer. If it is too thick,
add just a little water. Drizzle the sauce over the meat.

Serves 4

Steak Louisiana with
PEPPER, MUSHROOMS AND OKRA

4	beef tenderloin steaks (6 oz each), ¾-inch thick
4	large garlic cloves, minced
2 tbsp	ground black pepper
3 tbsp	olive oil
1 tbsp	balsamic vinegar
½ lb	mushrooms, halved
¼ lb	fresh okra, tipped and topped, sliced into ¼-inch rings
¼ cup	dry red wine

Rub the steaks well with the garlic. Put them and any loose garlic into a dish. Mix together the olive oil and balsamic vinegar and drizzle over the steaks. Cover with plastic food wrap and allow to stand at room temperature for half an hour, turning the steaks several times.

Lift the steaks from the marinade and rub well with the pepper. Use all the loose garlic left in the dish and the oil and vinegar mixture to fry the steaks in a medium frying pan. Fry at medium to high heat for 2 to 3 minutes a side or until they are browned. Remove the steaks and set aside.

Add the mushrooms to the frying pan and sauté until heated. Stir in the okra and sauté for 5 minutes more. Add the wine and simmer until the sauce thickens, which okra juices will naturally do.

Return the steaks to the pan. Cover and cook only until the steaks are heated through.

Serves 4

Okra is used extensively in Louisiana; I always recommend fresh okra for its flavour and texture.

Most people think that Louisiana cooking is very spicy. This is just one recipe that proves it's not.

Veal stew
with peppers and onions

A light, but spicy stew. Veal has a lighter flavour than beef and because it doesn't take as long to become tender the stew cooks more quickly. Another simple dish to prepare. Boil some potatoes and dinner is made.

2 lbs	1-inch thick veal steaks
1 1/2 cups	pecan halves
1/4 cup	butter
2 tbsp	olive oil
	flour
4	large garlic cloves, minced
1	small white onion, chopped fine
1	small red bell pepper, chopped
3 tbsp	sweet hot sauce (e.g., Tiger Sauce)
1 tbsp	mustard powder
1 tsp	balsamic vinegar
1 tsp	ground black pepper
	hot water

Melt the butter in a deep, medium frying pan. Stir in the olive oil, add the pecans and sauté for 3 to 5 minutes, making sure the butter does not burn. Remove the pecans with a slotted spoon and set aside.

Cut the veal into 1-inch cubes. Lightly dust the cubes in the flour and brown in the frying pan. Add the garlic, onion and red pepper. Sauté for 5 minutes. Stir in the sweet hot sauce, dry mustard, balsamic vinegar and pepper. Add just enough hot water to make a sauce, cover and cook over low heat for about 45 minutes or until the veal is very tender. Stir often and add more water if needed.

Stir in the pecans and cook for two minutes.

Serves 4 to 6

GEORGIA PEACH lamb chops

4	loin lamb chops (3 oz each)
1 tbsp	ground black pepper
¼ tbsp	salt
1 cup	pecans, lightly toasted
½ cup	fine bread crumbs
½ tbsp	garlic granules
2	sprigs fresh mint
½ cup	butter, melted
1 tbsp	olive oil
1	medium white onion, diced
2	canned peach halves
2 tbsp	peach yogurt
1 tbsp	minced fresh parsley

Toast the pecans in a 350° F oven.

Purée the pecans, bread crumbs, garlic and mint in a food processor until the pecans are as fine as the bread crumbs. Remove and place in a shallow bowl or dish.

Combine the pepper and salt and rub them into the lamb chops. Dip each chop into the melted butter and coat with the pecan mixture by pressing the chops into the pecans.

Heat the olive oil in a medium frying pan. Sauté the chops on medium heat until golden brown on each side. Transfer to a cookie sheet in a single layer and place in the oven to keep warm.

Add the onions to the frying pan and sauté until limp, picking up all the browned particles off the bottom of the pan. Lower the heat and push the onions to one side.

Place the peaches cut-side down in the open area of the frying pan. Cover the pan and cook for 2 to 4 minutes until the peaches are warmed through.

Arrange equal amounts of the onion on each of two dinner plates and put two lamb chops on top of the onion. Place a peach half cut-side up next to this. Spoon 1 tablespoon of yogurt into the centre of each peach and sprinkle with parsley. Serves 2

Lamb and fruit have always made a great combination. I preserve my own peaches, which are almost as good on a winter day as fresh peaches are in the summer. If you don't have home preserves, buy the best canned peaches you can find.

This recipe was passed on to me by friends in Douglas, Georgia.

Lamb shanks
roasted with vegetables

For a long time lamb shanks had to be ordered from a butcher shop, but you can now find them at supermarkets. As with all dishes that require a long simmering or braising, watch to make sure that all the liquid does not evaporate. Have some extra chicken broth on hand in case you need it.

8	small lamb shanks
1	large lime
1/2 tbsp	ground black pepper
1/2 tsp	salt
5 tbsp	olive oil, divided
1	large white onion, coarsely chopped
6	garlic cloves, coarsely chopped
1	medium celery root, sliced into strips
4	large carrots, sliced into strips
3 cups	chicken broth
1 tbsp	ground black pepper (or to taste)
1 tbsp	coriander powder
2 tbsp	chopped fresh cilantro
1/2 tbsp	thyme powder

Preheat oven to 375°F. Place the shanks in a non-metallic dish. Halve the lime, squeeze the juice over the shanks and rub them with the pulp. Sprinkle with the salt and pepper and set aside. Coarsely chop the spent lime and set aside.

Heat 3 tablespoons of the olive oil in a heavy-bottomed roasting pan on the stove. Add the onion and sauté over medium heat until tender. Stir in the garlic and sauté for 5 minutes. Add the celery root and carrots and sauté for 2 to 3 minutes. Remove the vegetables to a bowl with a slotted spoon and set aside.

Add the remaining 2 tablespoons olive oil to the roasting pan. Raise the heat to medium high and brown the shanks well on all sides. Push the spent lime pieces below the shanks, pour the chicken broth over and around the shanks and sprinkle with the remaining spices. Return the vegetables to the roasting pan, cover and bake for 2 hours.

Lower the oven temperature to 325°F and bake until the shanks are tender and the meat falls away from the bone, about 1 hour longer.

Serve right out of the roasting pan along with some boiled potatoes. Serves 4

Lamb chops MONTENEGRIN

8	loin lamb chops (3 oz each)
1/4 cup	dried and crushed red chilies
1/3 cup	and 2 tbsp olive oil
2 tbsp	fresh lime juice
6	large garlic cloves, chopped
3 tbsp	cumin powder
1 tbsp	coriander powder
1/2 cup	mayonnaise

Begin this dish the day before you plan to serve it. The long marinating period is an unusual treatment of lamb.

As are many dishes from Montenegro, this is on the spicy side.

Prepare the marinade by puréeing the red chilies, 1/3 cup olive oil, lime juice, garlic, cumin powder and coriander powder in a food processor. Combine the mayonnaise and the 2 tablespoons olive oil in dish large enough to hold the chops. Add the puréed ingredients and blend well.

Put the lamb chops in the dish and coat them evenly with the marinade. Refrigerate for 12 to 24 hours, turning the chops several times.

The following day, broil the chops until browned, about 3 to 4 minutes a side. Baste each side with the marinade once.

Serves 4

PORK medallions with
red bell peppers and asparagus

At one time I got a bargain on pork tenderloins, but I had to buy a 30-pound case. After a while when we were pretty tired of pork tenderloin in all the old familiar treatments, Pat suggested I incorporate asparagus and roasted bell peppers, two of our favourite vegetables.

1	pork tenderloin (¾ lb), membrane removed
	flour
3 tbsp	olive oil
	ground black pepper
½ cup	shallots, sliced
1 cup	roasted red bell peppers, in ¼-inch strips (see p 152)
½ tbsp	dried and crushed red chilies
½ tsp	salt
1 bunch	fresh asparagus, cut into 1 ½-inch lengths
¼ cup	water
3 tbsp	V8 Vegetable Cocktail

Slice the tenderloin crosswise in 1-inch-thick slices. Place one piece at a time between wax paper and pound the rounds with a meat mallet to approximately twice their original size.

Heat the olive oil in a medium frying pan. Dust the medallions in flour and sauté in the oil until well browned. You may have to do this in two batches.

When cooked, place the medallions in a dish, sprinkle with pepper, cover with plastic food wrap and set aside.

Sauté the shallots in the frying pan (a little more oil may be needed) until limp, making sure to scrape up all the browned meat particles. Stir in the red bell peppers and the red chilies and sauté for 5 minutes more. Gently stir in the asparagus and cook for 2 minutes. Transfer the vegetables to a bowl and cover with plastic food wrap.

Return the pork medallions to the frying pan in even layers. Mix the water and V8 juice together and pour over the meat. Arrange the vegetables over top, cover and simmer over low heat for 5 to 8 minutes

Gently remove the vegetables from the frying pan, placing them in the centre of a large, deep-dished serving platter. Arrange the pork medallions around the vegetables. Ladle any liquid over top.

Serves 2

TURKEY, CHICKEN & GAME HENS

Turkey breast jambalaya
with chorizo

In this recipe I've taken an old-time southern dish and I've substituted turkey breast and chorizo sausage for the usual leftover turkey and sausage. I like basmati rice for its flavour but any long-grain rice could be used.

1 lb	turkey breast, cut into 1-inch cubes
1 lb	chorizo sausage, sliced ⅛-inch thick
3 tbsp	butter
1	onion, minced
3	stalks celery, minced
1	large leek, minced
1	red bell pepper, diced
2	large garlic cloves, minced
½ cup	chopped fresh parsley
3 tbsp	chicken bouillon granules
2 tbsp	ground black pepper (or to taste)
1 tbsp	dried and crushed red chilies
1 tbsp	butter
1 ½ cups	chicken broth
1 cup	red wine
2 cups	basmati rice

Heat the olive oil in a large pot. Sauté the turkey pieces until browned, remove and set aside. Sauté the onion, celery, leeks and bell pepper in the pot until tender. Stir in the chorizo sausage, garlic and parsley. Sauté for 8 minutes more.

Return the turkey pieces to the pot. Gently stir in the chicken bouillon granules, pepper and red chilies. Add the butter, chicken broth and red wine and simmer for 5 minutes.

Return to a rolling boil. Stir in the rice, cover and cook for 20 minutes or until the rice is done, stirring occasionally.

Serves 4 to 6

CHICKEN GUMBO
Creole

1	chicken (3 lbs), cut into serving pieces
3 tbsp	bacon fat
2 lbs	fresh okra, cut into ½-inch rings
1	medium onion, diced
½ tsp	cumin powder
½ tsp	coriander powder
2 tbsp	flour
4	large plum tomatoes, skinned and diced
¼ cup	minced fresh parsley
3 tbsp	thinly sliced and chopped prsut or prosciutto
1 tsp	dried and crushed red chilies
	hot water

When this dish is cooked in Louisiana or Texas, one of the main ingredients is a cured, air-dried ham called tasso. I replace it with prsut or prosciutto which can be bought at European delicatessens where I live. Fresh okra is key; canned or frozen won't do the trick. Serve gumbo with rice.

Heat the bacon fat in a deep, medium frying pan. Sauté the chicken pieces until they are well browned on all sides. Remove with a slotted spoon and set aside.

Add the okra and onion to the pan and sauté over medium heat until they begin to brown. Stir in the cumin and coriander, sautéing for 2 minutes more. Remove the vegetables with a slotted spoon and set aside.

Pour off all but 3 tablespoons of fat. On medium heat, stir in the flour and sauté, creating a dark brown roux. Return the chicken pieces to the pan and ladle the onion and okra mixture over top. Add the tomatoes, parsley, ham and red chilies and just enough hot water to cover all the ingredients. Cover the pot and simmer over low heat for 1 to 1 ½ hours. Shake the pan several times to ensure that the ingredients are not sticking to the pan.

Serves 4

CAJUN CHICKEN STEW

HOT ELEMENTS · 110

When Pat and I were travelling around Louisiana, we tasted a lot of country cooking in little cafés. At home, I tried to copy some of the dishes. With this recipe, I think I came very close to what I remember eating. I serve it with rice.

6	boneless chicken breast halves, skinned
1/3 cup	olive oil
3 tbsp	flour
3/4 cup	chopped onion
4	large garlic cloves, minced
2	medium jalapeño peppers, seeded and minced
1 tbsp	grated fresh ginger
1 1/2 cups	chopped red bell pepper
1 1/2 cups	chopped yellow bell pepper
6	large plum tomatoes, skinned, seeded and coarsely chopped
2 1/2 cups	chicken broth
1	large banana, mashed
6	unpeeled red potato nuggets
6	unpeeled white potato nuggets
2 tbsp	minced fresh cilantro

Preheat oven to 325° F.

Combine the spice rub ingredients and dredge the chicken pieces in the rub.

Heat the olive oil in a large frying pan and sauté the chicken pieces until they are golden brown. This will take 3 to 4 minutes a side. Transfer the chicken pieces to a baking dish large enough to hold them in a single layer. Cover tightly with plastic food wrap to keep warm. You may have to do this in several stages to cook all the chicken pieces.

Stir the flour into the oil in the frying pan and sauté over medium heat, creating a brown roux. Add the onion, garlic, jalapeño, ginger, any remaining spice rub and the red and yellow peppers. Sauté for 10 minutes. Stir in the tomatoes and chicken broth, bring to a low simmer and cook for 10 minutes. Add the banana. When the sauce begins to simmer, gently spoon it over the chicken pieces.

Cover the pan with aluminum foil and place in the oven.

WITH BANANAS

While the chicken is in the oven, boil the unpeeled potatoes until tender. Drain them and cut into quarters. When the chicken has been in the oven for 45 minutes, remove the foil and sink the potato pieces into the sauce. Return the pan to the oven without the foil and cook only until the sauce begins to bubble.

Serves 4

Spice Rub

1 ½ tbsp	salt
1 tbsp	chili powder
1 tsp	paprika
1 tsp	cumin powder
1 tsp	turmeric powder
1 tsp	coriander powder
1 tsp	cardamom powder
1 tsp	granulated garlic
1 tsp	granulated onion
1 tsp	white pepper

Chicken baked with blood oranges

This baked chicken dish is on the lighter side and is enlivened by the citrus of the limes and blood oranges. Blood oranges from Florida and California appear in our stores from December to February.

2	chicken breasts, skinned and split
4	chicken thighs, skinned
4	chicken legs, skinned
2	large limes
3 tbsp	olive oil
	flour
1 tsp	salt
1 tbsp	ground black pepper (or to taste)
¼ cup	brown sugar
2	blood oranges, peeled and sliced very thinly
3 tbsp	water

Preheat oven to 350° F.

Grate the limes and set the zest aside.

Place the chicken pieces in a bowl. Squeeze the juice of the limes over top and rub each piece with the juice.

Heat the olive oil in a medium frying pan. Dust the chicken pieces in flour and sauté in the oil until well browned. Remove with a slotted spoon and transfer to a baking dish large enough to contain the pieces in one layer.

Combine the lime zest, salt, pepper and brown sugar. Sprinkle over the chicken pieces. Arrange the orange slices over top in several layers if necessary. Pour the water down the side of the dish. Cover and bake for 45 minutes.

Serves 4

Curried chicken with
TOMATO and FIG

2	chicken breasts, skinned and split
4	chicken thighs, skinned
4	chicken legs, skinned
⅓ cup	flour
1 tsp	ground black pepper
1 tsp	salt
3 tbsp	butter
2 tbsp	olive oil
½ cup	diced white onion
3	large garlic cloves, minced
2 tsp	curry powder
½ tsp	coriander powder
½ tsp	thyme powder
1 can	(14 oz) plum tomatoes, chopped with the juice
¼ cup	minced dried figs
3 tbsp	sunflower seeds, toasted

I like to serve this one right out of the frying pan. The dried figs add a delightful sweetness to this curry.

Combine the flour, salt and pepper and dredge the chicken pieces well in this mixture.

Heat the butter in a large frying pan until hot. Sauté the chicken pieces until well browned on both sides. Remove with a slotted spoon and set aside.

Add the olive oil to the pan, stir in the onion, garlic, curry powder, coriander and thyme. Sauté over low to medium heat, scraping up all the browned chicken bits off the bottom of the pan.

Stir in the chopped tomatoes and juice, cover and simmer for 5 minutes.

Return the chicken to the frying pan, bone-side down. Replace the lid and simmer over low heat for 30 to 40 minutes.

Stir in the figs, cover and remove from the heat. Allow to stand for 5 minutes. Sprinkle with the toasted sunflower seeds and carry the frying pan to the table.

Serves 4

CHICKEN AND MUSHROOM wrap

Once when B.C. Gas asked Pat and me to do cooking shows on four consecutive days, I set out to create one recipe that would be simple and easy. I had some chicken thighs in the freezer, bought some mushrooms and tortillas, and this recipe was born. It was a huge hit with the audience, B.C. Gas and ourselves.

1 lb	chicken thighs, skinned and boned
1 lb	mushrooms, diced
½ cup	minced onions
3 tbsp	olive oil
	flour
½ cup	barbecue sauce (e.g., The Fire Chef)
¼ cup	water
8	corn tortillas

Heat the olive oil in a medium frying pan. Dredge the chicken pieces in the flour and fry until well done and golden brown. Remove from the pan, cut into bite-size pieces and set aside.

Sauté the mushrooms and onions in a medium nonstick frying pan without oil until the mushrooms are rendered down and have released all their liquid. This will take about 8 minutes.

Add the chicken pieces to the mushrooms in the non-stick pan and cook until heated through. (Using a nonstick pan will keep the chicken from browning further.) Combine the barbecue sauce and water. Add to the pan and stir well. Cook this over medium heat until the sauce begins to thicken and caramelize.

Warm the tortillas in the oven or a tortilla steamer. Place equal amounts of chicken and mushrooms on each tortilla and wrap.

Serves 4

Cornish game hens AFIRE

1	large Cornish game hen, halved
3 tbsp	olive oil
2 tbsp	dried and crushed red chilies
1 tsp	ground black pepper
1 tsp	coriander powder
½ tsp	salt
2	large limes

This is a very hot treatment of a generally mild-tasting meat. To reduce the heat, don't use the dipping sauce.

Preheat oven to 350° F.

Prepare the sauce by combining the olive oil, red chilies, pepper and coriander.

Place the two halves of the hen in a bowl, pour the sauce over top and hold at room temperature for no longer than half an hour. Baste with the sauce several times.

Put the hen pieces, skin-side up, in a baking dish. Pour the sauce over top and place in the oven for one hour. Raise the heat to 425° F and bake until the skin is well browned and crisp. Remove the hen to a serving platter.

Add the juice of the two limes and the salt to the baking dish. Bring the liquid to a simmer, scraping up any browned bits off the bottom of the dish. If your baking dish can't be heated on a stove, transfer everything in the dish to a small saucepan and heat. Put the sauce into a small bowl for dipping.

Serves 2

TURKEY DINNER
with all the stuff and NO MUSS

HOT ELEMENTS · 116

The biggest complaint about cooking a turkey dinner is the fuss of the last hour when you make gravy, mash potatoes, cook another vegetable and carve the bird. There are pots and pans everywhere. You are away from your family or guests, and the cleanup is a horror. My plan makes work beforehand but pays off in a clean kitchen and time to sit down and relax before serving dinner.

Read these instructions twice. They aren't as difficult as they appear at first. They certainly are much easier than what you have been doing for years.

The turkey

  1 turkey (18 lbs), washed

For years, I stuffed the turkey the night before roasting it. Now, recognizing the hazards in that procedure, I make some preparations for the stuffing beforehand – chopping the vegetables and tearing up the bread into chunks – but I do the final combining of ingredients and the stuffing of the bird just before I'm going to cook it.

Don't neglect to remove the neck and giblets from the turkey. Although some people make a stock from them, I don't.

The stuffing

3 lbs	lean ground pork
2½ cups	chopped fresh parsley
2½ cups	minced leeks, white ends only
2½ cups	finely chopped celery hearts
6 cups	dry bread chunks
3½ cups	whole milk
4	large eggs
⅓ cup	poultry seasoning, or your own combination of herbs
	fine bread crumbs

Let the turkey come to room temperature while you prepare the stuffing.

Soak the bread chunks in the milk. Combine the pork, parsley, leeks, celery and bread chunks in a large bowl. Blend in the eggs. Add the fine bread crumbs, a little at a time, until the stuffing gets stiff and easy to work with.

Stuff the bird and set it on a roasting rack in a shallow roasting pan.

The cooking time will be about 7½ hours, plus a resting period of 40 or so minutes. You will want to put the turkey in the oven about 8 hours and 15 minutes before you plan to sit down to dinner.

Potatoes, oranges and olives in a salad (p 122)

Nectarine topping (p 144)

Roasting the turkey

        salt

        black pepper

1 lb bacon slices

Preheat oven to 325°F.

Sprinkle the bird with salt and pepper and place a strip of bacon on each drumstick and wing. Use the remainder to cover the breasts. Tent the bird with aluminum foil and place in the oven. I don't baste the turkey at all.

    After 3 hours, add 2 cups of hot water to the roasting pan.

    After 6 hours, remove the turkey from the oven and discard the aluminum tenting. Lift the turkey from the pan and transfer it to a disposable aluminum roasting pan. Remove the bacon and discard. Return the bird to the oven and continue to roast until done. (Take the bird's temperature by inserting an instant-read thermometer into the thickest part of the thigh.)

The perfect gravy

While the turkey finishes roasting, you have enough juice in the original pan to make the gravy.

2 tbsp olive oil

3 tbsp butter

7 tbsp flour

1 tsp ground black pepper

2 cups chicken broth

Heat the olive oil and butter in a medium saucepan. Stir in the flour and sauté over medium heat, creating a brown roux. Remove from the heat and set aside.

    Remove as much of the fat as you can from the original roasting pan but keep all the juice and browned bits. Place the roasting pan over medium heat. Add the chicken broth and bring to a simmer, scraping up all the browned bits off the bottom and sides of the pan. Simmer for 5 minutes and then strain. Again, separate any fat from the liquid.

    Return the roux to low to medium heat and stir in the strained liquid from the roasting pan, stirring constantly. If needed, add a little hot water to reach the consistency you prefer for gravy. Stir in the pepper, simmer for 3 minutes and set aside.

    Wash the original roasting pan and put it away.

Serves 8

Preparing the vegetables

While the turkey is roasting, cook Brussels Sprouts Pan-fried with Spices (page 135), Mashed Baked Potatoes (page 134) and Carrots in a Honey Ginger Sauce (page 136), doubling each of the recipes. When the Brussels sprouts and carrots are cooked, transfer them to a serving bowl, cover with plastic food wrap and set aside. Transfer the potatoes to a baking dish.

Wash the cooking pots and put them away.

When the turkey is done, remove it from the oven. Place on a cutting board, tent well with plastic food wrap and allow it to sit for 30 to 40 minutes before slicing. You may have to remove juice that accumulates under the turkey.

Remove the plastic food wrap from the potatoes and heat them in the oven as directed.

Now is the time to relax with your family and friends. The rest is easy.

Serving the vegetables

On a low power in the microwave, reheat the Brussels sprouts for 5 to 7 minutes. Remove the plastic food wrap and toss very gently.

On a low power in the microwave, reheat the carrots for 5 to 7 minutes. Remove the plastic food wrap and toss gently.

Remove the potatoes from the oven.

Reheat the gravy and place in a gravy boat.

Carving the turkey

Remove the food-wrap tent. Cut off the drumsticks and wings, placing one of each at both ends of a large serving platter. Remove both breasts and thighs, slice them on a cutting board and arrange in the centre of the platter. Remove the stuffing and place in a serving bowl.

Carry all the dishes to the table for serving.

Later, put the carcass of the bird in a resealable plastic bag in your freezer to use for turkey soup.

Discard the aluminum foil pan. Theoretically, you will have only one pot to wash – the one used for the gravy. It and your dinner dishes should all fit into your dishwasher.

Happy holidays!

SALADS & SIDE DISHES

Romaine **salad** supreme

My untossed Caesar salad without the usual raw egg and the croutons. The dressing uses lime juice instead of lemon. The inner romaine leaves are generally sweeter than the dark outer leaves.

1	large romaine lettuce heart
6	large garlic cloves, minced
4	anchovies, minced, then mashed
1/2 cup	olive oil
2 tbsp	fresh lime juice
1 tbsp	vinegar
1 tbsp	balsamic vinegar
1 tbsp	ground black pepper (or to taste)
1/2 tsp	salt
1/3 cup	freshly grated Parmesan

Prepare the dressing by combining the anchovies, olive oil, lime juice, vinegars, pepper, salt and cheese in a jar. Cover with a lid and shake well to blend.

Quarter the romaine heart, lengthwise, being careful to keep the quarters intact. Put one quarter on each of four salad plates. Carefully cut across the quarters, at one-inch intervals, leaving them looking intact.

Shake the dressing and drizzle equal amounts over each salad serving.

Serves 4

AVOCADO in a lime vinaigrette

3	large avocados, peeled, pitted and coarsely diced
2	medium limes
1 tsp	raspberry vinegar
1 tsp	sugar
1/2 tsp	ground black pepper
1/4 tsp	salt

Place the avocados in a shallow salad bowl. Add the juice of the limes, the raspberry vinegar, sugar, pepper and salt. Gently toss and refrigerate for 30 minutes. Toss the salad several times.

Allow the salad to sit at room temperature for 10 minutes, toss gently and serve.

Serves 4

Raspberry vinegar is a pleasing combination with avocado. Because avocado quenches the heat of chilies, serve this salad with or after a spicy dish.

Potatoes, oranges and olives
in a salad

This may sound a little too different, but it's a tasty and attractive combination. A pepita is a type of pumpkin seed. If you can't find them, use salted sunflower seeds.

16	small new white potatoes
2	oranges, peeled and chopped
1½ cups	kalamata olives
1 cup	chopped green onions
½ cup	chopped celery leaves
¼ cup	olive oil
2 tbsp	fresh lime juice
1 tbsp	raspberry vinegar
½ tsp	sugar
¼ tsp	coriander powder
	salt
	ground black pepper
2 tbsp	salted pepitas, lightly toasted

Boil the potatoes for 10 minutes, remove from the heat and allow to stand in hot water for 15 minutes. Cool the potatoes under cold water.

When the potatoes are cool, cut them into quarters and put into a bowl. Add the oranges, olives, green onions and celery leaves and toss gently.

Combine the olive oil, lime juice, raspberry vinegar, sugar and coriander in a jar and shake well to blend.

Pour the dressing over the potatoes, cover with food wrap and refrigerate until ready for use but toss several times.

An hour before serving, take the salad from the refrigerator arrange it on a large serving platter. Sprinkle with salt, pepper and the toasted pepitas.

Serves 4

COLESLAW
with Memphis hot sauce dressing

½ head	green cabbage, very finely sliced by hand
1	large carrot, grated
1	small onion, minced
2 tsp	vinegar
1 tsp	ground black pepper
¼ tsp	salt
⅔ cup	mayonnaise
2 tbsp	sugar
1½ tsp	mustard powder
1 tsp	hot sauce (e.g., Melinda's XXXtra Hot Sauce)

My recipe is loosely based on types of coleslaw I have eaten in Tennessee. Prepare this one several hours ahead of time, allowing the dressing to soften up the cabbage.

Place the cabbage, carrot and onion in a large bowl. Toss with the vinegar, pepper and salt. Refrigerate for 1 hour, tossing several times. Combine the mayonnaise, sugar, mustard powder and hot sauce. If the mixture is too thick, add a little cream. Ladle over the cabbage and toss well.

Serves 4

MELON SALAD
in a walnut dressing

½	honeydew
½	cantaloupe
1	large papaya
4 tbsp	minced fresh parsley
2 tbsp	minced fresh chives
3 tbsp	walnut oil
3 tbsp	olive oil
4 tbsp	fresh lime juice
⅓ tsp	ground black pepper
½ tbsp	Dijon grainy mustard
⅛ tsp	savory
⅛ tsp	thyme powder
⅛ tsp	tarragon powder
1 head	butter lettuce
	salt

Cut each fruit in half, remove the seeds, peel and cut into slices.

Place the fruit slices, parsley and chives in a large bowl. Gently toss and set aside.

Combine the walnut oil, olive oil, lime juice, pepper, grainy mustard, savory, thyme and tarragon in a jar. Shake well until blended.

Pour the dressing over the fruit, cover with plastic food wrap and refrigerate for 1 hour. Gently toss the fruit several times.

Line each salad bowl with 2 or 3 butter lettuce leaves. Spoon the fruits and the juices into the lettuce cups and sprinkle very lightly with salt.

Serves 4

Avocados with
cider vinegar and soy sauce

4	large avocados
¼ cup	hot water
2 tbsp	brown sugar
1 ½ tbsp	fresh lime juice
1 tsp	cider vinegar
½ tsp	soy sauce

Prepare the dressing by placing the water and sugar in a small jar, cover with a lid and shake to dissolve the sugar. Add the lime juice, cider vinegar and soy sauce and refrigerate to chill.

When you are ready to serve, cut the avocados in half and remove the pits. Using a small spoon, enlarge the pit hole to the skin. Put two avocado halves in each individual salad bowl. Stir the chilled dressing and ladle into the pit holes.

Serves 4

When I designed this combination, I didn't know if it was a salad or a dessert. Use it as you choose, either to build your appetite or to make a refreshing end to dinner.

salad dressings

When I want to get away from the usual oil and vinegar dressings, I can always count on one of these two recipes.

Olive oil with honey and mustard

4 tbsp	olive oil
1 1/2 tbsp	fresh lime juice
1 tbsp	Dijon mustard
1 tbsp	liquid honey
1/2 tsp	sesame seeds, lightly toasted
1/4 tsp	ground black pepper

Put all the ingredients in a bowl and whisk until well blended.

Yields enough for 4 servings

Honey, ginger and mustard dressing

2 tbsp	grainy mustard
1 tbsp	finely grated fresh ginger
1 tbsp	liquid honey
1 tbsp	Dijon mustard
3 tbsp	olive oil
2 tbsp	fresh lime juice
1 tbsp	sugar
1/2 tbsp	balsamic vinegar
1/2 tsp	ground black pepper
1/4 tsp	salt

Combine the grainy mustard, ginger, honey and Dijon mustard in a bowl. Slowly whisk in the olive oil. Whisk in the lime juice, sugar, balsamic vinegar, pepper and salt. Allow to stand at room temperature for half an hour before using.

Yields enough for 4 servings

Portabella MUSHROOMS
with cheese

4	medium portabella mushrooms
2 tbsp	olive oil
2	large garlic cloves, minced
1 tbsp	port wine
1/2 cup	freshly grated Parmesan

Preheat oven to broil.

Gently break off the stems of the mushrooms. Lightly brush the mushrooms clean.

Combine the olive oil, garlic and port wine in a small bowl. Put the mushroom caps, smooth-side up, on a broiling pan and broil until they begin to char ever so slightly.

Turn the caps, brush with half the olive oil mixture and broil for another 2 minutes.

Brush again with the olive oil mixture. Sprinkle each with cheese and broil for another minute or so, making sure that you do not burn the cheese.

Serves 4

Experts say these massive mushrooms were first cultivated in North America, while some people say they are of Italian origin.

They are one of the largest mushrooms with a rich, earthy taste. Vegetarians find they make a satisfying substitute for meat.

CAULIFLOWER
sautéed with spices

*Hints of the Orient
and the American
South, with
turmeric giving the
cauliflower a beauti-
ful golden yellow
colour.*

1 large cauliflower, cleaned and cut into medium florets
2 tbsp butter
1 tbsp olive oil
½ tbsp finely grated fresh ginger
1 large garlic clove, thinly sliced
½ tsp turmeric powder
½ tsp coriander powder
1 tsp cumin powder
½ tsp paprika
½ tsp mustard powder
½ tsp ground black pepper
½ tsp salt

Heat the butter and olive oil in a medium frying pan. Sauté the ginger and garlic over medium heat for 3 minutes. Add the turmeric and sauté until the mixture turns to bright yellow.

Add the cauliflower and shake and stir, making sure to coat all the florets.

Stir in the coriander, cumin, paprika, mustard, pepper and salt. Sprinkle with 2 tablespoons of water and cover with a tight-fitting lid.

When the steam has built, reduce the heat and simmer for 3 minutes. Remove the lid and sauté until all the moisture has evaporated from the pan.

Serves 4

leeks in an ORANGE glaze

6	small leeks, well washed
½ tsp	ground black pepper
	salt
¼ cup	frozen orange juice, not diluted
1 tbsp	olive oil
1 tbsp	balsamic vinegar
1 tsp	salted shelled sunflower seeds

When I prepared this simple dish on television, I had to make a second batch for the host and her crew to eat after the show.

Slice off the root end of the leeks and remove the outer layer. Discard the dark green tops, using only the white to light-green portions.

In a pot large enough to hold the leeks, bring water to a boil and cook the leeks for 3 to 5 minutes, depending on their size. Transfer the leeks to very cold water to stop the cooking process.

Slice the leeks in half, lengthwise and put them cut-side up in a baking dish, just large enough to hold them. Sprinkle with pepper and salt.

Gently heat the orange juice, olive oil and balsamic vinegar in a small saucepan. Spoon over the leeks and sprinkle with the sunflower seeds.

Broil in the oven until the leeks just begin to brown, being careful not to burn them.

Serves 4

Cornmeal

with butter and yogurt

In this recipe the yogurt really smoothes out the texture. This is the way I have most often eaten cornmeal. If you prefer it firm and sliced, add the butter and only half the yogurt. Cook and stir until the cornmeal begins to set. Invert on a cutting board, and allow to sit for 10 minutes. To cut, slide a piece of nylon thread under the slab and pull upwards.

1 cup	yellow cornmeal
1½ cups	cold water
¼ cup	butter
1 cup	yogurt

Combine the cornmeal and water in a large pot. Bring to a boil, lower the heat and cook on a low heat for 25 to 40 minutes, stirring often with a wooden spoon.

When the water has all been absorbed and the cornmeal has become a smooth porridge, stir in the butter and yogurt and cook over low heat for 5 minutes more.

Serves 4 to 6

Potato salad
Dalmatian-style

8	medium unpeeled Yukon gold potatoes
1 lb	bacon, fried crisp and crumbled
¼ cup	olive oil
3 tbsp	flour
1	large egg
¾ cup	cold water
¼ cup	white vinegar
¼ cup	sugar
2 tbsp	ground black pepper (or to taste)
1 tsp	salt
¼ tsp	cumin powder
¾ cup	minced green onions
¼ tsp	celery seed
	ground black pepper

In this unusual preparation of potato salad, you coat the potatoes with a cooked, spiced roux. The salad is best served at room temperature.

Cook the potatoes unpeeled. When they have cooled, peel and dice them and place in a large serving bowl.

Heat the olive oil in a medium saucepan. Stir in the flour and sauté over medium heat until you have a tan roux. Remove from the heat.

Lightly beat the egg and add the vinegar and water to it. Return the roux to the heat and slowly add the egg mixture, stirring constantly. Stir in the sugar, pepper, salt and cumin and bring to a low simmer. Continue to stir until the mixture is creamy-smooth. If it becomes too thick, add a little hot water.

Toss the green onions and celery seed gently with the potatoes and with just enough of the dressing to coat the potatoes well. Sprinkle with pepper and crumbled bacon. Serve at room temperature.

Serves 4

Carrots, radishes & cucumbers
sautéed

*An unlikely combi-
nation but one that
is a treat for the
tastebuds.*

10	small young carrots, cleaned
1	medium English cucumber, seeded and cubed
1 bunch	radishes, cleaned and halved
1 tbsp	butter
1/2 tbsp	olive oil
1/4 cup	minced fresh parsley
1/2 tsp	ground black pepper
1/4 tsp	dried whole Mexican oregano

Steam the carrots until tender, 5 to 8 minutes. Rinse under cold water and cut in half lengthwise.

Heat the butter and oil in a medium frying pan. Sauté the carrots, cucumber and radishes over medium heat until hot. Stir in the parsley, pepper and oregano and sauté for 3 minutes more.

Serves 4

RUTABAGA and carrot sweet mash

1	medium rutabaga, peeled and cut into 1-inch cubes
6	large carrots, peeled and cut into 1-inch rounds
½ cup	butter
¼ cup	brown sugar
1 tsp	ground black pepper

Put the rutabaga and carrots into a pot, cover with water and boil for about 15 to 20 minutes until they can be pierced with a sharp paring knife.

Drain the vegetables well, return to the pot and mash coarsely (not as smooth as mashed potatoes). Blend in the butter, sugar and pepper.

Serves 4

I had a similar dish prepared for me in the firehalls some 30 years ago. I loved it, but my children hated it. When I prepare it now, Pat and all our friends enjoy it, but my grown children still hate it.

Baked MASHED potatoes

Chicken broth replaces the usual milk in my mashed potatoes, and red chilies give an unexpected spark.

6 large unpeeled Yukon gold potatoes
1/2 cup butter
1/2 cup yogurt
2 tbsp minced fresh parsley
1/2 tsp ground black pepper
1/2 tsp salt
1/4 tsp dried and crushed red chilies
chicken broth
olive oil

Preheat oven to 350 °F.

Boil the potatoes in a large pot for 10 minutes. Turn off the heat and allow to stand for 15 minutes.

Drain the potatoes, remove the skins and return to the pot. Mash them well. Stir in 1/4 cup of butter, yogurt, parsley, black pepper, salt and red chilies.

If the potatoes are very thick, blend in some chicken broth a little at a time.

Grease a 9- by 12-inch baking dish with some olive oil. Spread the potato mixture into the dish, making small peaks over the entire top.

Put the dish in the oven. While it is baking, brush melted butter over the top, which should turn a light golden brown. Bake for 30 to 45 minutes.

(If you are making this dish in advance for my holiday turkey dinner, simply cover the mashed potatoes in the baking dish with plastic food wrap until it's time to remove the covering and bake as directed above.)

Serves 4

brussels sprouts

panfried with spices

20 Brussels sprouts, trimmed and halved lengthwise

4 large garlic cloves

1 tbsp and ¼ cup olive oil

1 tbsp butter

1 tsp ground black pepper

½ tsp salt

¼ tsp coriander powder

¼ tsp dried and crushed red chilies

¼ tsp dried whole Mexican oregano

1 tbsp fresh lime juice

½ tsp balsamic vinegar

½ tsp sugar

Some of the spices used in this recipe give a Mexican flavour. If you don't enjoy spicy food, omit the red chilies.

Wrap the garlic cloves tightly in aluminum foil and bake at 350°F for 30 to 40 minutes. Remove and set aside to cool.

Steam the Brussels sprouts over simmering water for 5 minutes. Drain and hold.

Heat the 1 tbsp of olive oil and the butter in a medium, nonstick frying pan. Sauté the steamed Brussels sprouts for 5 to 8 minutes, gently stirring or shaking the pan often. Add the pepper, salt, coriander and red chilies. Sauté for 3 minutes more. Crush the oregano between your fingers and sprinkle over the sprouts. Cover the pan, remove from the heat and allow to stand for about 5 minutes.

Prepare the dressing by blending the ¼ cup olive oil, lime juice, balsamic vinegar, sugar and the roasted garlic in a food processor or blender until creamy.

Put the sprouts in a bowl and drizzle the dressing over top. Toss gently.

(If you are preparing this recipe in advance for my holiday turkey dinner, cook the sprouts as above but do not apply the dressing. Transfer to a bowl that can go in the microwave. When the sprouts are cool, cover the bowl with plastic food wrap. Heat the sprouts and drizzle on the dressing.) Serves 4

Carrots sautéed in a honey and ginger sauce

Don't skimp on the ginger; it gives carrots a new meaning. If you're looking for a vegetable dish to add colour to your table, this is one.

2	bunches baby carrots, cleaned and washed
4 tbsp	liquid honey
2 tbsp	butter
½ tbsp	ground black pepper
½ tbsp	ginger powder
2 tbsp	minced fresh parsley
1 tbsp	raspberry vinegar

Cut the carrots, crosswise into bite-size pieces. Place in a medium saucepan, cover with water and boil until tender, but still firm. Drain well and transfer to a bowl. Cover and set aside.

Add the honey, butter, pepper and ginger to the saucepan. Cook over low heat just to melt the butter. Stir in the parsley and vinegar. Add the carrots. Cook over low to medium heat, just long enough to heat the carrots to their centres. Transfer to a warmed bowl.

(If you are preparing this dish in advance for my holiday turkey dinner, cook the carrots as above, put into a bowl that can go in the microwave. When the carrots have cooled, cover the bowl with plastic food wrap.)

Serves 4

DESSERTS & TREATS

Bananas FOSTER

I don't know who Foster is, but I encountered his dessert often in Arizona, Texas and New Mexico. It can be made earlier in the day. Allow to cool and cover. When it's time to serve, uncover and heat over low to medium heat for 3 to 5 minutes and serve as below.

3	large bananas
1/4 lb	butter
1 cup	Demerara sugar
1/3 cup	banana liqueur
1/4 tsp	cinnamon powder
1/4 cup	dark rum
	vanilla ice cream

Melt the butter in a deep, medium frying pan. Stir in the brown sugar, banana liqueur and cinnamon. Cook and stir over low to medium heat until all the sugar has dissolved and the sauce is at a low simmer.

Peel the banana and slice into ⅜-inch rounds. Add the banana rounds to the pan, cut-side down, and cook for 5 minutes. Turn the rounds over and cook for another 5 minutes. Gently spin the pan several times while cooking to make sure the banana isn't sticking to the bottom.

Drizzle the rum over top and carefully light it. Cook until the flame goes out. Stir gently and remove from the heat and allow to stand for 5 minutes.

Place a scoop or two of ice cream into four dishes. Portion out the bananas around each scoop and spoon the sauce over the ice cream.

Serves 4

Fritters
with yogurt and citrus zests

3 cups	yogurt
1 lb	flour
2	large egg yolks, beaten
1 tbsp	freshly grated lime zest
1 tbsp	freshly grated orange zest
1 tbsp	vanilla
1 tsp	baking soda
9 cups	(approximately) olive oil
	icing sugar

In my family, these were served as a dessert, an appetizer or for afternoon munchies. One to two cups raisins could be added to the fritters.

Combine the yogurt, flour, egg yolks, lime zest, orange zest and vanilla in a large bowl. Add the baking soda and blend well.

Heat about two inches olive oil in a deep, medium frying pan.

Take walnut-sized scoops of the dough and fry them until golden yellow. Remove with a slotted spoon to a large platter and sprinkle with icing sugar while still hot. Eat while hot or at room temperature.

Yields 40 to 70

Dixie's BANANA CAKE

A lady named Dixie gave me this recipe, and she really is from Alabama. This recipe makes three single-layer cakes, which you might dust with icing sugar for decoration.

4 large ripe bananas, mashed
1 1/2 cups sugar
1/2 cup vegetable shortening
2 large eggs, separated
1/2 cup buttermilk
1 tsp baking soda
1/2 tsp baking powder
1 tsp vanilla
2 1/2 cups flour

Preheat oven to 350°F.

Cream the sugar and shortening in a large bowl. Add the egg yolks and beat thoroughly. Stir in the buttermilk, baking soda, baking powder and bananas, mixing very well. Add the vanilla and egg whites, again mixing well.

Blend in the flour and pour into 3 greased and floured 9-inch-square cake pans. Bake for 25 to 30 minutes.

Texas mango bread

with raisins and walnuts

2 cups	diced mango
2 cups	flour
1 1/2 cups	sugar
2 tsp	baking soda
2 tsp	cinnamon powder
1/2 tsp	ginger powder
1/2 tsp	salt
3	large eggs
3/4 cup	vegetable oil
1/2 cup	raisins
1/2 cup	walnuts, chopped
1 tbsp	fresh lime juice

This quick bread is a variation of a recipe I found in Texas.

Preheat oven to 350°F.

Lightly grease and flour two small loaf pans (4 1/2 by 8 inches).

Combine the flour, sugar, baking soda, cinnamon, ginger and salt in a bowl. Lightly beat the eggs and stir them and the vegetable oil into the flour mixture. Blend in the raisins, walnuts and lime juice. Pour the batter into loaf pans. Bake for approximately 1 hour or until a toothpick inserted into the centre of the loaf comes out clean.

Pear and blueberry CRISP

5	large firm pears, peeled and sliced
1 cup	fresh blueberries
1/3 cup	sugar
1 tbsp	fresh lime juice
1/4 tsp	cinnamon powder
1/4 tsp	nutmeg powder
	butter

Preheat oven to 350°F.

Combine the fruits, sugar, lime juice and spices and toss gently. Butter a casserole dish, add the mixture and level the top with a rubber spatula.

Topping

1/2 cup	flour
1/2 cup	rolled oats
3/4 cup	brown sugar
1/2 tsp	cinnamon powder
1/2 tsp	ginger powder
1/2 cup	butter, cold

Combine the flour, oats, brown sugar, cinnamon and ginger. Using a pastry blender or your fingertips, incorporate the butter until the mixture becomes crumbly. Sprinkle over top of the fruits and bake for 45 minutes or until the top is golden brown.

Mama's Palačinka

DESSERT CRÊPES

3	large eggs
¼ tsp	salt
1 tbsp	powdered sugar
¾ cup	flour
1 cup	buttermilk
1 ½ tbsp	butter, melted
	olive oil

Fill these crêpes with plain cottage cheese or fresh minced fruit and sprinkle with icing sugar just before serving.

Beat the eggs, salt and sugar in a bowl. Slowly stir in the flour and buttermilk, add the melted butter and blend well.

Heat a nonstick crêpe pan over medium to high heat and brush with olive oil.

Ladle approximately ¼ cup of the batter into the pan, tilting the pan to spread the batter over the entire area. Cook for about 40 seconds. The top of the crêpe should lose its shine, and the bottom will be a light tan colour.

Transfer to a plate and continue cooking crêpes until all the batter is used.

Spread a tablespoon or so of your favourite filling over the crêpe. Roll it up and top with a fruit sauce, such as my Nectarine Topping.

Yields about 12

Nectarine topping

Use this topping on crêpes, vanilla ice cream or sponge cake. I think that nectarines are one of the most flavourful fruits and enjoy cooking with them. People are surprised that I put pepper with fruit but it is a combination that works.

4	large ripe nectarines
1/3 cup	butter
1/2 cup	Demerara sugar
1 tbsp	fresh lime juice
1/2 tbsp	ground black pepper (or to taste)

Halve the nectarines and remove the pits. Peel and slice each of the halves into 6 to 8 wedges, depending on their size.

Melt the butter in a medium nonstick frying pan. Stir in the sugar and cook over low to medium heat for 2 to 3 minutes. Add the wedges of nectarines, lime juice and pepper. Cook about 10 minutes, gently stirring and turning the nectarines until the liquid in the pan becomes syrupy.

Serves 4

PRUNE cake

1 cup	pitted prunes
2 cups	flour
1 tsp	baking soda
1 tsp	nutmeg
1 tsp	cinnamon
1 tsp	salt
2 cups	sugar
2	large eggs
½ cup	olive oil
1 cup	liquid, from the cooked prunes
1 tbsp	fresh lime juice
¾ cup	chopped pecans
	icing sugar

My mother was a fantastic cook, but she did not bake a lot of desserts. Those she made were wonderful, but my sister, brother and I learned as kids that if we really raved about something, we seldom saw it again. This is one of those.

Preheat oven to 350°F.

Place the prunes in a medium saucepan and just cover with water. Simmer until tender. Remove with a slotted spoon. When cool, chop fine. Measure 1 cup of the prune juice.

Mix together the flour, baking soda, nutmeg, cinnamon and salt in a bowl. Stir in the minced prunes.

Beat the sugar, eggs and oil in a mixer at high speed until mixed well.

Using a spoon stir the flour mixture into the eggs. Fold in the lime juice and the prune juice until just blended.

Pour into a 13 by 9 by 2-inch greased and floured pan and sprinkle with the nuts.

Bake at 350°F for 40 to 45 minutes or until a toothpick comes out clean.

Cool in the pan. When cool sprinkle with icing sugar and cut into bars.

Knedle od sljive

(Dumplings with stewed plums)

Traditionaly a whole plum is wrapped in a potato dough, simmered in water and then dredged in the bread crumb mixture. My variation makes the whole process easier.

10	large European plums
	sugar
¼ cup	butter
¼ tsp	salt
¼ tsp	fresh lime zest
2	eggs
¼ lb	cottage cheese, drained well
2 cups	2- or 3-day old white bread, crust removed and diced very fine
¼ cup	sour cream
½ cup	flour
½ lb	butter
¼ cup	olive oil
2 cups	fine bread crumbs
1 tbsp	sugar

Pit and mince the plums, place in a medium saucepan and cook over a low heat for about 1 hour. Add sugar to taste.

To make the dumplings, cream the ¼ cup of butter, salt and lime zest until fluffy. One by one beat in the eggs. Add the cottage cheese, diced bread and sour cream. Beat well. Finally beat in the flour until well blended. Chill for at least one hour so that the batter has a chance to stiffen.

Have some salted water boiling in a stock pot. Using a small wet teaspoon form the batter into small dumplings and cook in one batch gently in the water for 15 minutes.

While the dumplings are cooking, brown the bread crumbs by heating the ½ pound butter and olive oil in a medium frying pan until the butter has melted. Add the bread crumbs and 1 tablespoon of sugar, sautéing until the crumbs are lightly browned. If it is too thick, add a little more olive oil.

When the dumplings are cooked, remove them from the water with a slotted spoon and drain well. Dredge in browned bread crumbs. Serve warm with the stewed plums. Serves 4

Maralynn's
chocolate chip cookies

2 cups	butter
1 cup	brown sugar
1 cup	white sugar
2	large eggs
1 tsp	vanilla
2 cups	rolled oats
2 cups	flour
1/2 tsp	salt
1 tsp	baking soda
1 tsp	baking powder
12 oz	chocolate chips
1	Hershey chocolate bar (4 oz), grated
1 1/2 cups	walnuts, chopped and lightly toasted

This recipe was given to me by Maralynn Elder, who is the secretary at the Training Division of the Vancouver Fire and Rescue Service.

Preheat oven to 375°F.

Put the rolled oats in a blender or food processor and process them to a fine powder.

Cream the butter and both sugars in a large bowl. Add the eggs and vanilla, mixing them well. Add the powdered oats, flour, salt, baking soda and baking powder and again mix well.

Stir in the chocolate chips, grated Hershey bar and nuts, blending all the ingredients well.

Roll into balls and place on a cookie sheet about 2 inches apart. Bake in the oven for 10 minutes at 375°F.

Yields about 50

MY HOMEMADE SAUCES & STAPLES

The Making of a ROUX

Many of my Cajun and Croatian recipes call for a roux, which most of us associate with French cooking even though the same process under a different name appears in many southern European cuisines. In Croatia for instance, a roux is an *ajmpren* (pronounced i'm-pren).

A roux is butter, oil or other fat blended with flour and sautéed over low to medium heat. When combined with a liquid, a roux will thicken sauces, soups, chowders and gravies.

If cooked for only a few minutes, a roux will be white or blond but the longer the fat and flour cook, the darker the roux will become and the stronger, more nutty, its flavour. Cream sauces, soups and chowders call for white to blond roux. For gravies, soups, dark sauces and the gumbos and jambalayas of Creole cooking, the roux may be anywhere from a tan to a dark mahogany.

Increasing in darkness, the colours I call for are white, light blond, tan, dark brown, mahogany and dark mahogany.

A white roux is usually made with equal parts butter and flour; the darker roux use olive oil and flour, sometimes but not always, in equal proportions.

To make a perfect roux, heat the oil or butter over medium heat in a heavy-bottomed pot or frying pan. Add flour equal in quantity to the oil or butter and sauté until the mixture becomes the colour you want. This will take some care and almost constant stirring.

For soups, chowders and gumbos, use ¼ cup olive oil with 2 to 3 tablespoons flour to thicken from 2 to 4 quarts of liquid. For sauces, use ⅓ cup olive oil with 4 tablespoons flour to thicken 2 to 3 cups of liquid.

Béchamel sauce

4 tbsp	butter
2 1/2 tbsp	flour
1/2 cup	chicken broth
1/2 cup	whipping cream
1/4 tsp	salt
1/8 tsp	nutmeg powder

Melt the butter in a heavy-bottomed saucepan. Stir in the flour and sauté over medium heat, creating a light blond roux. Gradually, stir in the chicken broth and cream. Cook until the sauce becomes thick and creamy. Add the salt and nutmeg. Simmer for 2 minutes and remove from the heat.

Yields 1 cup

Garlic mustard sauce

This sauce goes with anything, and as you can see there is no major shopping or work involved.

6	large garlic cloves, not peeled
3	egg yolks
4 tbsp	fresh lime juice
1 tbsp	balsamic vinegar
1 tbsp	mustard powder
1/2 tsp	salt
1/2 tsp	seasoning salt
1 cup	olive oil (more or less)
1 tsp	ground black pepper
1 tsp	dried whole Mexican oregano

Place the garlic cloves in a small saucepan, cover with water and bring to a boil. Rinse under cold water and slip the cloves out of the husks into a food processor. Purée with the egg yolks, lime juice, balsamic vinegar, mustard powder, salt and seasoning salt. With the appliance running, slowly drizzle in as much olive oil as you need to make a smooth sauce. Turn off the appliance, scrape down the sides, add the pepper and oregano and blend for just a few seconds longer.

Yields about 1 cup

Roasting RED BELL PEPPERS

Several brands of bottled roasted red bell peppers are available in supermarkets.

While red bell peppers are generally chosen for roasting, the other bell peppers and chili peppers are also delicious when roasted because they take on a sweeter, more pungent flavour. They can enhance salads, sauces, pasta dishes and do wonders to burgers.

Peppers may be charred over a hot stove element but I find that a messy procedure. I prefer oven broiling.

Preheat oven to 500°F.

Cut the stems out with a sharp knife. With a teaspoon, scrape out as much of the ribs and seeds as you can. Wash well to remove any remaining seeds and allow to drain.

Place aluminum foil on the rack below the one on which you will be placing the peppers. Put the peppers directly on the rack, close the oven door and turn the oven to broil.

When the peppers are charred, turn them with tongs. Continue to broil and char until they are done on all sides, about 8 to 10 minutes. Place in a resealable plastic bag, seal and allow to stand for 10 minutes. Remove and put in a bowl until cool to the touch.

Holding the peppers over the bowl to collect all the oil and juices, peel off all the charred skin. Your roasted peppers are ready for use.

For later use, put the peppers and the collected juices in a glass jar and cover with olive oil. Put a tight-fitting lid on the jar and store in the refrigerator for 3 to 5 weeks.

Red bell pepper sauce

2 cups	roasted red bell peppers, homemade (page 152) or purchased
1 cup	chicken broth
2	large leeks, white ends only, minced
1 cup	plain yogurt
1 tbsp	celery salt
1/4 tsp	cayenne pepper

Bring the chicken broth and leeks to a boil in a saucepan, lower the heat and simmer for half an hour. Stir in the bell peppers and simmer for 5 minutes more. Allow the mixture to cool before putting it into a blender or food processor with the yogurt. Process until puréed. Remove to a bowl and stir in the celery salt and cayenne pepper. Refrigerate for an hour before using.

Yields about 3 cups

Tomato olive salsa

1 tbsp	butter
1/4 cup	very thin onion slices
1/4 cup	very thin red bell pepper slices
1 tsp	flour
1 tsp	chili powder
1/4 tsp	cayenne pepper
1/4 cup	sliced pitted black olives
1/4 cup	sliced pitted green olives
1 cup	chopped canned plum tomatoes

Melt the butter in a saucepan. Sauté the onion and bell pepper until limp. Stir in the flour and sauté for 3 to 5 minutes. Add the chili powder, cayenne pepper, black and green olives and tomatoes. Cook for 5 minutes. If the salsa is too thick, stir in a little V8 juice or water.

Yields 2 cups

Salsa with tomato and cilantro

Although cilantro is not one of my favourite herbs, it does enhance this salsa. Adjust the amount of cilantro to please your palate.

1 tbsp	olive oil
¼ cup	white onion, minced
1	small red bell pepper, cleaned, seeded and diced
½ cup	dry red wine
1 can	(14 oz) plum tomatoes, drained and chopped
⅓ cup	coarsley chopped fresh cilantro
1 tbsp	ground black pepper
1 tsp	salt
1	large lime

Heat the olive oil in a frying pan. Sauté the onion and bell pepper until limp. Add the wine and simmer until the liquid is reduced by half.

Stir in the tomatoes, pepper and salt, simmering for about 20 minutes until the mixture thickens. Blend in the cilantro and squeeze the lime juice over top. Will keep under refrigeration for 2 days.

Yields about 2 cups

Fresh tomato salsa

4	large plum tomatoes, peeled and diced
1	medium white onion, diced
½ cup	minced green onions
2 tbsp	salsa seasoning spice (e.g., Watkins)
1 tsp	ground black pepper

Combine all the ingredients in a bowl and refrigerate for 4 hours or overnight. Toss several times. Bring to room temperature before serving.

Yields 1 ½ cups

DARN-IT'S-HOT
salsa

10	large tomatoes, peeled and chopped
4	large red bell peppers, seeded and chopped
6	large jalapeño peppers, seeded and chopped
3	medium onions, chopped
6	large garlic cloves, minced
½ cup	tomato paste
½ cup	V8 Vegetable Cocktail
¼ cup	vinegar
¼ cup	natural cane sugar
1 tbsp	salt
1 tbsp	paprika
1 tbsp	coriander powder
1 tbsp	dried and crushed red chilies
½ tbsp	dried whole Mexican oregano
⅓ cup	minced fresh cilantro

Here is a salsa that you prepare in a large batch and process in jars in a boiling-water bath. More work than a fresh salsa, but perhaps enough to last you for the season.

Heat the tomatoes, bell peppers, jalapeño peppers, onions, garlic, tomato paste and V8 juice in an 8-quart pot. With the exception of the cilantro, stir in the remaining ingredients and bring to a boil. Reduce the heat to a low simmer and cook and stir often until the mixture thickens.

To see if the salsa is thick enough, dab 1 tablespoon on a smooth dinner plate. Slowly tilt the plate. The salsa should not run freely but move very slowly, sticking to the plate. If it is too runny, return to the heat and simmer until it passes the tilt test. Blend in the cilantro and simmer, stirring often, for 10 minutes.

Ladle into sterilized canning jars, leaving a ¼-inch headspace. Screw the lids on firmly.

Have a canning kettle ready with enough boiling water to cover the jars. Lifting the jars with tongs, put them on the rack in the kettle, not touching one another. Bring the water to a boil for 15 minutes.

When stored in a cool place, this salsa will keep for months. Refrigerate after opening. Yields 8 to 10 cups

Cuban spice sauce

Hot but also flavourful and a great dip for a beef or pork fondue. In a sealed container, it can be kept under refrigeration for up to a month.

¼ cup habanero chili peppers, seeded and minced
¼ cup green chili peppers, seeded and chopped
2 tbsp fresh lime juice
1 tbsp vinegar
1 tbsp balsamic vinegar
1 tbsp chopped fresh cilantro
½ tbsp cumin powder
2 garlic cloves, minced
1 tsp salt
½ tsp ground black pepper

Purée all the ingredients in a food processor. The sauce should be about the same consistency as a high-quality mustard. If it is too thick, add more lime juice, a little at a time.

Yields about ¾ cup

Montenegro dipping sauce

First you make the spicy Montenegro sauce and then blend as much of it as your palate can tolerate into mayonnaise. Keeps well under refrigeration.

⅓ cup dried and crushed red chilies
¼ cup olive oil
4 anchovy fillets
1 tbsp fresh lime juice
4 large garlic cloves, minced
3 tbsp cumin powder
¾ cup mayonnaise
1 tbsp olive oil

For the Montenegro hot sauce: Sauté the chilies and olive oil in a small saucepan over low heat for about 5 minutes. Purée in a food processor with the anchovy fillets. Combine the puréed mixture with lime juice, garlic and cumin in a bowl.

Blend together the mayonnaise and 1 tablespoon olive oil in a dipping bowl. Stir in some of the Montenegro hot sauce, a little at a time until you reach an acceptable heat level.
Yields about 1 cup

Seafood cocktail sauce

Serve with steamed shrimp, prawns or crab meat. This sauce gains flavour when prepared 1 or 2 days in advance.

3 tbsp	ketchup
2 tbsp	Dijon grainy mustard
1 ½ tbsp	lime juice
1 ½ tbsp	hot horseradish
1 tbsp	Mexican paprika
2	large garlic cloves, chopped
1 tsp	hot sauce (e.g., Melinda's XXXtra Hot Sauce)
½ tsp	ground black pepper
½ cup	olive oil

Purée all the ingredients except the olive oil in a food processor. With the appliance running, slowly drizzle the oil into the mixture. Transfer to a bowl, cover with food wrap and refrigerate to chill.

Yields about 1 cup

Cucumber yogurt sauce

Served as a side dish with curry or any other spicy meal, it does a superb job of mellowing heat or tartness.

2	large English cucumbers, peeled and grated
1 tbsp	fresh lime juice
½ tsp	salt
½ cup	yogurt
¼ cup	2 per cent milk
1 tbsp	minced green onion
½ tbsp	ground black pepper

Combine the cucumber, lime juice and salt in a bowl, cover with food wrap and refrigerate for 1 hour. Drain the cucumbers and gently blend in the yogurt, milk, green onion and pepper. Cover with food wrap and return to the refrigerator. This sauce should be chilled and tossed lightly before serving.

Yields 3 cups

Sweet hot mustard

An excellent condiment for a ham or corned beef dinner.
Keeps well under refrigeration.

¹⁄₂ cup	brown sugar
¹⁄₄ cup	mustard powder
1 tbsp	flour
2	eggs, beaten
¹⁄₃ cup	water
¹⁄₃ cup	fresh lemon juice
2 tbsp	balsamic vinegar

Combine the sugar, mustard powder and flour in a saucepan. Add the beaten eggs and whisk until smooth. Add the water, lemon juice and vinegar and place on medium heat. Cook and stir until the sauce becomes thick and creamy.

Store in the refrigerator. This sweet hot mustard will keep for up to 2 months.

Yields about 1 cup

Cranberry relish

It's the pepper that distinguishes this quick and easy condi-
ment for game meats and poultry. It may be stored in the
refrigerator for up to seven days.

3 cups	canned jellied cranberries
2	large oranges, peeled,
1 cup	brown sugar
1 cup	frozen orange juice, undiluted
2 tbsp	ground black pepper (or to taste)

Peel the oranges and remove the white membrane from them and their rinds. Place the oranges and rinds in a food processor, add the cranberry jelly and brown sugar, blending until smooth. Transfer to a saucepan and bring to a low simmer. Stir in the orange juice and pepper and simmer for 5 minutes. Serve at room temperature.

Yields 4 cups

Some staples I Buy

- Bertolli Olive Oil: virgin not extra-virgin, which I find too heavy.

- Curry Powder: I order mine from Pendery's Inc., 1221 Manufacturing Street, Dallas, Texas, 75207.

- Gebhardt Chili Powder: one of the finest blends, which I buy in 5-pound bottles. Available in 3-ounce and 11-ounce sizes from Secrets to Cooking Tex/Mex, 2864 Silverhills Road, Crestview, Florida 32536 (http://www.texmex.net).

- Melinda's XXXtra Hot Sauce: a blend of peppers, carrots, onion and lime juice; flavourful and not vinegary.

- Old Bay Seasoning: good with seafood and poultry.

- Sonoma Marinated Tomatoes: naturally dried and packed in olive oil; supple and tasty.

- Tellicherry Black Pepper: the ultimate black pepper; you can taste the difference.

- Tiger Sauce: fairly hot and a little sweet.

- V8 Vegetable Cocktail: for many sauces and soups, it is lighter and less dominant than tomato juice. It makes a good virgin Caesar for Sunday brunch.

- Whole Mexican Oregano: not as overpowering as Mediterranean oregano.

Index